Human Nature in the Bible

William Lyon Phelps

Human Nature in the Bible

Copyright © 2013 by Bibliotech Press
All rights reserved.

Contact:
BibliotechPress@gmail.com

The present edition is a reproduction of 1922 publication of this work. Minor typographical errors may have been corrected without note, however, for an authentic reading experience the spelling, punctuation, and capitalization have been retained from the original text.

ISBN: 978-1-61895-125-0

CONTENTS

Introduction	1
I. The Creation and the Flood	3
II. Four Great Personalities—Abraham, Isaac, Jacob, Joseph	12
III. Moses and the Ten Commandments	25
IV. Famous Fighters in Canaan	39
V. Ruth, Eli, Samuel, Jonathan and King Saul	50
VI. King David	61
VII. Solomon in all His Glory—The Romantic Figure of Elijah	75
VIII. The Prophet Elisha	89
IX. Downfall of Israel and Judah—The Patriotic Stories of Daniel and Esther	104
X. The Apocrypha	120
XI. Wisdom and Philosophy—Proverbs and Ecclesiastes	137
XII. Human Nature Revealed in Poetry—Job, Song of Songs, Psalms, Isaiah	152

INTRODUCTION

Priests, atheists, sceptics, devotees, agnostics, and evangelists are generally agreed that the Authorised Version of the English Bible is the best example of English literature that the world has ever seen. It combines the noblest elevations of thought, aspiration, imagination, passion and religion with simplicity of diction.

Everyone who has a thorough knowledge of the Bible may truly be called educated; and no other learning or culture, no matter how extensive or elegant, can, among Europeans and Americans, form a proper substitute. Western civilisation is founded upon the Bible; our ideas, our wisdom, our philosophy, our literature, our art, our ideals, come more from the Bible than from all other books put together. It is a revelation of divinity and of humanity; it contains the loftiest religious aspiration along with a candid representation of all that is earthly, sensual and devilish. I thoroughly believe in a university education for both men and women; but I believe a knowledge of the Bible without a college course is more valuable than a college course without the Bible. For in the Bible we have profound thought beautifully expressed; we have the nature of boys and girls, of men and women, more accurately charted than in the works of any modern novelist or playwright. You can learn more about human nature by reading the Bible than by living in New York.

The Elizabethan period—a term loosely applied to the years between 1558 and 1642—is properly regarded as the most important era in English literature. Shakespeare and his mighty contemporaries brought the drama to the highest point in the world's history; lyrical poetry found supreme expression; Spenser's *Faerie Queene* was a unique performance; Bacon's Essays have never been surpassed. But the crowning achievement of those spacious times was the Authorised Translation of the Bible, which appeared in 1611. Three centuries of English literature followed; but although they have been crowded with poets and novelists and essayists, and although the teaching of the English language and literature now gives employment to many earnest men and women, the art of English composition reached its climax in the pages of the Bible.

The translators made more mistakes in Greek than they did in English. When we remember that English is not a perfect language, for as a means of expression it is inferior to both Russian and Polish, it is marvellous to consider what that group of Elizabethan scholars did with it. We Anglo-Saxons have a better Bible than the French or the Germans or the Italians or the Spanish; our English translation is even better than the original Hebrew and Greek. There is only one way to explain this; I have no theory to account for the so-called "inspiration of the Bible," but I am confident that the Authorised Version was inspired.

Now as the English-speaking people have the best Bible in the world, and as it is the most beautiful monument ever erected with the English alphabet, we ought to make the most of it, for it is an incomparably rich inheritance, free to all who can read. This means that we ought invariably in the church and on public occasions to use the Authorised Version; all others are inferior. And, except for special purposes, it should be used exclusively in private reading. Why make constant companions of the second best, when the best is available?

The so-called Revised Version and modern condensed versions are valuable for their superior accuracy in individual instances; they may be used as checks and comments; but for steady reading, and in all public places where the Bible is read aloud, let us have the noble, marbly English of 1611. I suggest that one reason why so many people cease reading the Bible after childhood, is because most copies are printed in abominably thin and small type. It is easy to obtain a Bible in convenient shape and weight, printed in large, black type, which pleases the eyes instead of destroying them.

In this book I shall consider the Old Testament as a work of literature, revealing the grandeur, the folly, the nobility, the baseness of human nature. I shall not consider it primarily as "the history of the Hebrew people," for the Hebrew people are much like other people, having the same passions, impulses, purity, filth, selfishness and self-sacrifice that dwell side by side in the heart of every man and woman in the world. I shall consider it as I would a play, an essay, a novel, a poem. The characters in the Bible are just as real to me as Theodore Roosevelt. I shall therefore point out and try to interpret interesting and significant episodes and passages, with one hope in the back of my mind all the time—that those who read these pages will re-read the Bible with renewed zest.

W. L. P.

Yale University,
Tuesday, 22 *August*, 1922.

I

THE CREATION AND THE FLOOD

The Beginning—God the Supreme Artist—The Fourth Day—The River—Adam and Eve—The Power of Choice—The Triple Curse—Cain and Abel—Long-lived Ancestors—Methuselah—The Flood—Noah— Noah's Wife—Drunkenness of Noah—His Curse

The early chapters of Genesis are a kind of Outline of History, like that by H. G. Wells, only better written. They are even more condensed than his, and like his book, they attempt to account for the things we see: light, the sun, moon, stars, land, water, animals, and man. No one knows how any of these came into existence, but the Bible account is sublime in its simple dignity, and begins in a reasonable and orderly manner by putting the First Cause first. I have read accounts of the origin of the world in the bibles of other religions, and they all, while containing some fine and interesting remarks, seem to have much that is trivial and silly. There is nothing childish or silly in our Bible. The narrative opens like a great symphony:

In the beginning God created the heaven and the earth.
And the earth was without form and void; and darkness was upon the face of the deep. And the Spirit of God moved upon the face of the waters.
And God said, Let there be light; and there was light.

Lotze said that the Mosaic cosmogony was more sublime than any other, and he was right. It represents physical changes coming from the Divine Will, coming easily and immediately. The control of mind over matter seems to me more natural and reasonable than the other way around, in spite of the fact that some reasonable men are materialists. In the last analysis the idea that the human mind developed out of matter seems to me as curious as the idea that an automobile should make a man, rather than a man make an automobile. I wonder if those who believe that thought, imagination, poetry and music were made by matter do not fall into a vicious circle by somehow thinking that the creative matter had mind in it.

Although it is impossible for the mind of man to understand the mind of God, I can, in a minute fashion, appreciate the happiness of God as He surveyed each day's achievement. "God saw that it was good," and rejoiced. Of course He did. One of the features of the Bible account of creation is that it represents God as the Supreme Artist. The world has always loved great artists—In books, paintings, buildings, statues, and music. One reason why I love God is because the beauty of the universe came from Him. He made the sun and stars, the mountains, the sea, the trees, and the flowers. Joyce Kilmer said:

Poems are made by fools like me,
But only God could make a tree.

The first chapter of Genesis represents the Artist in the full glow of creation. As He made Light, Water, and Land, He stopped to survey His work, and He felt a thrill of joy. There is no doubt that some of the highest and purest happiness known to man is when he finishes a painting or a poem or a symphony that he knows is good; and the Bible is undoubtedly right when it represents the greatest of all Artists looking on His creations with delight. As Aprile said to Paracelsus:

God is the perfect poet, Who in His person acts His own creations.

Aprile was a poet and knew what he was talking about. After a life of dissipation he found his way to God through beauty as others have found it through character. Furthermore, there is something divine in the act of creation. Beethoven, Raphael, and Shakespeare seem in some mysterious manner to approach divinity.

As a representation of continuous masterpieces in art, such as an artist throws off in his happiest moods, the first chapter in the Bible has a magnificence all its own; from the point of view of science it marks the procession from the inorganic to the organic; the waters were divided, the lower waters receded, and the dry land appeared; then came vegetation, luxurious, abundant—the third day. Fish and fowl appeared on the fifth day; on the sixth came the beasts of the earth, running and creeping flat, followed by the upright figure of man.

The only thing in the six days' progression which seems to me strange is the creation of the sun, moon, and stars on the fourth day. In Dostoevski's novel, *The Brothers Karamazov,* this is mentioned, together with an illustration of how obedience in a pupil used to be more highly regarded than intelligence. When Smerdyakov was twelve years old, Grigory began to teach him the Bible. "But the teaching came to nothing. At the second or third lesson the boy suddenly grinned. 'What's that for?' asked Grigory, looking at him threateningly from under his spectacles. 'Oh, nothing. God created light on the first day and the sun, moon, and stars on the fourth day. Where did the light come from on the first day?'......'I'll show you where!' he cried, and gave the boy a violent slap on the cheek."

Doubtless the boy then saw more stars than were in the lesson. Violence is a convenient but not permanent method of silencing questions. Furthermore, there have been plausible answers to Smerdyakov's query.

I remember in studying Latin grammar at school I exclaimed: "I don't see the use of learning these strings of exceptions by rote."

The teacher flew into a rage and shouted: "Your business is not to ask questions, but to do the work assigned to you."

I then believed the teacher to be mistaken; now I know he was.

And the Lord God planted a garden eastward in Eden; and there he put the man whom he had formed.

And out of the ground made the Lord God to grow every tree that is pleasant to the sight, and good for food; the tree of life also in the midst of the garden, and the tree of knowledge of good and evil.

And a river went out of Eden to water the garden.

I can see the pleasant river flowing through the greenery. It is interesting to remember that the Bible begins and ends with a river. The earthly paradise and the heavenly were each beautified by a noble river; see the first verse of the last chapter in the Bible. Curious that so many Christians have believed in a river of death, when there is no suggestion of it in the Bible, where is described the river of life. The Styx has no place in Christian theology; yet many Christians talk of crossing the river of death, perhaps because Bunyan made such a dramatic scene of it in the *Pilgrim's Progress*. It may have annoyed him that he could not give chapter and verse for it, his usual method of fortifying his pictures and anecdotes.

Adam does not appear to have been remarkable either for intelligence or for courage; but he must have been extraordinarily ingenious. He named all the animals. In language he must have had creative ability and a large vocabulary. Anyone who wishes to know what a mental feat this literary branding was has only to try to name six things in a row. The late Mr. Pullman gave one of his daughters a large salary simply for naming each new Pullman car. Was it she who made them sound like a list of *dramatis personae* in Shakespeare?

John Donne, who was Dean of St. Paul's three hundred years ago, seems to have admired Adam's verbal skill, for in his Fourth Satire, describing a man he met at court, he says he saw

A thing it would have posed Adam to name.

The creation of Eve completed the beauty of the scene, for there is nothing lovelier than a lovely woman in a lovely garden.

Hir yelow heer was broyded in a tresse,
Bihynde hir bak, a yerde long, I gesse,
And in the gardin, at the sonne up-riste,
She walketh up and doun, and as her liste
She gadereth floures, party whyte and rede,
To make a sotil gerland for hir hede,
And as an aungel hevenly she song.

Between them, and with some prompting, Adam and Eve managed to ruin the garden, as has been man's way with Nature ever since. Browning said, "Heaven's gift takes earth's abatement." One does not have to read ancient history to see what man has done with Nature's gifts of richness and beauty. Look around now and consider.

Regarding the old story, perhaps the most amazing thing bestowed on our first parents was the gift of choice. It seems astounding that they had it entirely within their own power to destroy their happiness. They were as unfitted for the elective system in life as most of their descendants have been, but their destiny was placed within their control, and they naturally chose wrong. To put the tree of life and the tree of knowledge within their reach seems like putting sugar and arsenic within the grasp of children; the situation has not materially changed within the last six thousand years. Adam and Eve were distinctly warned in advance, which had the natural effect; today moderns have all the advantages that come from humanity's collective wisdom, and with what result?

Adam and Eve did not know by previous experience what would happen. How much wiser are we? Every commencement essay in schools and colleges upholds a sufficient number of moral ideals to save the world, based on knowledge, and are all graduates saints? We know exactly what is bad for us, and then we take it.

Recently we have been taught something of the results of war on a large scale, although we are only beginning to feel them. We are solemnly warned what the "next war" will mean. Now does anybody seriously believe that there will not be another war?

What the fowls of the air and the beasts of the field looked like in the Garden of Eden I really do not know, but it is impossible to mistake Adam and Eve. They were one hundred percent human. They were the average man and woman of 1922. The American poet, Vachel Lindsay, impliedly defines Democracy in the phrase, "The people have a right to make their own mistakes." Well, no development is possible without the power of choice; and human history begins with it.

The snake was a practiced liar; but his chief lie was not in saying, "Ye shall not surely die," although this was, like everything else he said, a lie; his chief lie was in the remark, "Ye shall be as gods, knowing good and evil," the very passage that Mephistopheles, disguised as the Doctor, wrote in the student's book in Faust. We should substitute the words "men and women" for "gods"; for it is humanity that knows by sad experience the difference between good and evil, whereas the serene gods of most nations have been either beyond all such boundaries or indifferent to their possible import.

The garden of Eden resembled modern society both in the existence of sin and in its punishment. There the punishment was not long delayed. When the sin was discovered, it must be confessed that Adam did not present a very chivalrous attitude; he "told on" his wife immediately, like a coward at school. "And the man said, The woman thou gavest to be with me, she gave me of the tree, and I did eat." Is it possible that in the first clause of Adam's reply there is a hint of irony as well as of plaintiveness?

What was the punishment? What was the curse? To Adam hard labour. "In the sweat of thy face shalt thou eat bread." He must become a farmer, which is in the twentieth century not a popular profession. Furthermore, he would get his food with difficulty. The earth would yield a good crop only by toil and eternal vigilance; whereas weeds would rise spontaneously. "Thorns also and thistles shall it bring forth to thee." This curse has not yet been lifted.

The curse to Eve? She will bear children in bodily anguish, and she will be subordinate to her husband: "he shall rule over thee." Apparently in the garden of Eden, before they ate of the tree, Adam and Eve enjoyed absolute equality. During the last century the daughters of Eve have made strenuous efforts to nullify this part of the curse. Partly owing to inferiority in physical strength, they have not yet wholly succeeded. Physical inferiority was a curse apparently provided particularly for women; in animal life females are often on a par with males in speed and strength, and there are those who believe they are even more deadly.

The curse to the snake? He was to become an object of eternal loathing to men and women. And, except to professional snake-charmers and to some strange-minded children, he is still an object inspiring horror, dread, and hate.

It is always tragic to leave one's home forever, much harder on the woman than on the man. I am sure that Eve felt worse than Adam as they fared forth into the wilderness. Perhaps the emotions of both were accurately guessed by Milton in the noble close of *Paradise Lost:*

They, looking back, all the eastern side beheld
Of Paradise, so late their happy seat,
Wav'd over by that flaming brand; the gate
With dreadful faces throng'd, and fiery arms.
Some natural tears they dropt, but wip'd them soon;
The world was all before them, where to choose
Their place of rest, and Providence their guide:
They hand in hand, with wandering steps and slow,
Through Eden took their solitary way.

History is largely the record of the killing of man by man; birds are protected by law, and a few of them may be shot only in the open season; whereas just as many men are killed in one month as in another. And in times of war there is no closed season. The first murder occurs in the fourth chapter of the Bible, indicating again how speedily man began to be true to himself. Abel was a keeper of sheep, but Cain was a tiller of the ground. No wonder Cain was ill-tempered. He had to drive oxen, whereas Abel merely sat and watched the peaceful sheep. It is said by professional plowmen that it is almost impossible to drive oxen without swearing; and certainly tillers of the soil often become fluent in this manner of speech. Cain seems to have had a violent temper anyhow, which was not improved by the day's work. He also had a Tom Sawyer hatred for good little boys; and perhaps Abel's piety and blamelessness became insufferable. Apparently the murder was not deliberately planned, but was the result of a sudden, overmastering impulse. It is interesting to observe that Cain was permitted to live, branded as much for safety as for disgrace; and it is still more interesting to note that his great-great-great grandson, Lamech, was also a murderer. Whom he killed or why he did it we shall never know; but he regretted it, for he remarked to his two wives: "I have slain a man to my wounding and a young man to my hurt."

Human responsibility was the law that Cain broke: his surly remark, "Am I my brother's keeper?" has come echoing down the ages, and received a final answer in our Lord's parable of the Good Samaritan. The rebellious element in Cain's nature has made him a hot favourite with many poets, who turned him into a hero of drama, Byron's Cain arousing the attention of Europe. But Cain was really no hero; he was simply very human. He seems more real than his mild brother. Cain's descendants were important pioneers; the murderer Lamech had three sons—Jabal, the cowboy; Jubal, the musician; Tubal-Cain, the smith. It is pleasant to see, so early in history, music placed on an apparent equality with more "useful" and philistine work.

The patriarchs that followed our first parents seem to have lived long. Adam set a good example by living nine hundred and thirty years; hard work and plenty of fresh air were no doubt good for him. Perhaps they did not begin to feel old till they had passed their eighth century; I have a suspicion that when they were about eight hundred and fifty they resented the attitude of striplings of three hundred-and-so, who tried to help them on with their cloaks —"I'm just as young as I ever was." Methuselah was the champion, living to be nine hundred and sixty-nine; but, after all, in excitement his life may have been shorter than Rupert Brooke's.

When I was a child I heard Mark Twain deliver a graduating address at school. He said: "The subject of my remarks is Methuselah; he lived to be nine hundred and sixty-nine years; but what of that? There was nothing doing." Methuselah would have been interested could he have known that when he passed the record set by Jared, who lived nine hundred and sixty-two years, he would be famous so long as there is a man left on the earth. Few men in history are more of a household word today; and Bernard Shaw is the latest to make use of his name in literature. I suppose the women lived as long as the men, though their ages are not recorded. Sarah's age was given much later and for a special reason.

There were giants in the earth in those days, mighty men which were of old, men of renown; so we learn in the sixth chapter of Genesis; but from the moral point of view they were not mighty at all.

And God saw that the wickedness of man was great in the earth, and that every imagination of the thoughts of his heart was only evil continually. And it repented the Lord that he had made man on the earth, and it grieved him at his heart.

The first of these two verses is not an exaggeration and—with reservations— would do fairly well for any period of human history; the second takes us back to the First Day, when God saw that it was good. Nature was splendid, human nature evil— where every prospect pleases, and only man is vile. The earth needed a bath, and got it.

The story of the Flood, as given in Genesis, is dramatic in its simplicity. It is one of the best short stories ever written; no child, hearing or reading it once, will forget it in maturer years—the building of the dreadnought ark; the entrance of Noah, his wife, his three sons—Shem, Ham, Japheth—with their wives; the dignified procession of animals, two by two.

In the Bible account there seem to have been no domestic difficulties when the rain began to fall; Noah, his wife and family, all entered the ark without any urging. But in the mediaeval Mystery Plays, where the flood was naturally a favourite scene, humour was injected into the story. Noah's wife had an unpleasant disposition, and emphatically refused to have anything to do with the ship. She finally consented to enter if the ladies' club to which she belonged might come in too; Noah was naturally unable to comply with this demand. While Shem, Ham, and Japheth are leading all the animals into the steerage, Noah's wife, although the waters are rising and the situation seems desperate, regards the exertions of her husband and sons with cynical disdain.

Noye. Wiffe, come in: why standes thou their?
   Thou arte ever frowarde, I dare well sweare;
   Come in, one Codes name! halfe tyme yt were,
   For feare leste that we drowne.

Noyes Wiffe. Yea, sir, sette up youer saile
   And rowe fourth with evill haile,
   For withouten fayle
   I will not oute of this towne;
   But I have my gossippes everechone
   One foote further I will not gone;
   The shall not drowne, by Sante John!
   And I may save ther life.

Noah is perplexed and evidently not for the first time; the sons speak rather roughly to their mother, except Japheth, the gentleman, who entreats; all to no avail. Then Shem picks her up, throws her into the boat, and as Noah says doubtfully, "Welcome, wife, into this boat," she strikes him with her fist. This slap-stick farce delighted our British ancestors.

In a time when few could read, the mediæval stage helped to keep the Bible alive.

At the deluge Noah was in the prime of life, a middle-aged man, *un homme mur,* being six hundred years old. After the event he lived three hundred and fifty years, dying at the age of nine hundred and fifty. How frequently during those remaining three centuries and a half Noah and his family must have talked about the flood! It could hardly be said to have been a landmark in their history, but I can imagine them using it as a great date. "That happened before the flood." "Do you remember three hundred years after the deluge, when I broke my hip?"

I wonder what the constitution of the water was during the complete submersion. Did the ocean make the whole expanse salt, or did the mighty rain make the sea fresh? This, like the song of the Sirens, or what name Achilles took at the girls' school, we shall never know.

No child brought up on the Bible—as all children should be—ever forgets the happy moment when the waters "asswaged"; and "in the tenth month, on the first day of the month, were the tops of the mountains seen." The sending out of the raven and then the dove appeals to the imagination; I have often wondered how long it took the mates of these two birds to find them. On the second trip of the dove her fluttering at the window of the ark in the evening, bearing the olive leaf in her mouth, must have caused enormous conversation within the family circle inside. After six days on the water, green fields are a thrilling sight; what must this olive leaf have signified to the weary voyagers?

The absolute persistence of sin on the earth is the cardinal fact in human history; all the ocean and all the rain could not wash wickedness off the land. Although Noah knew that the inhabitants had been slain because of their evil doing, and although he and his family had been miraculously spared, and although he had built an altar and worshipped as soon as he touched the ground, almost his next recorded act was to get drunk. It was like going to church in the morning and getting drunk in the afternoon—still a familiar sight in certain parts of the world. Perhaps after so much water, wine seemed attractive.

Ham had the misfortune to see his father dead drunk; and Noah, when he awaked, instead of being penitent for his disgrace, cursed his son for seeing him. Noah is not the only person in history who felt worse about being caught than about doing wrong. I never was favourably impressed by Noah's cursing his own son; of course he was in a bad temper when he woke up and probably had a desperate headache; but if he had said, "Lord, be merciful to me a sinner!" I should have had more respect for him than when he added to the sin of drunkenness the sin of cursing his own child, just like a drunken *paterfamilias!* His cursing his son did more harm than he intended; for the text, "Cursed be Canaan," was a favourite basis for many sermons in Southern churches in America, eloquently delivered in support of the institution of human slavery. I wonder why so many ministers deem it their duty to support the dominant political party from the pulpit, instead of preaching the gospel.

II

FOUR GREAT PERSONALITIES

The Destruction of Sodom—Character of Lot—Lot's Wife—The Laughter of Abraham—The Sacrifice of Isaac and Its Repetition in the Twentieth Century— Isaac's Mother—Courtship of Rebekah—Jacob's Treachery to Esau—The Vision in the Night—Joseph and His Brothers—Joseph in Egypt—The Great Recognition Scene

We learn that because of its wickedness, the population of the earth, with the exception of one family, was destroyed by cloud-bursts; the twin cities of the plain, Sodom and Gomorrah, were destroyed by a rain of fire and brimstone, and they seem to have deserved extinction. Lot, Abraham's nephew, is an interesting person; he was a man of business, shrewd and clear-headed, hospitable and fair-spoken, but not religious like his distinguished uncle; he was a man of the world. He prospered so abundantly that even in those broad lands the passion of earth-hunger, which has caused so many devastating wars, started a small fight between his herdsmen and those of Abraham. This might have led to serious consequences but for the wisdom and forbearance of the man of God. Abraham suggested that perhaps there was room enough in the world for both, and generously gave Lot the first choice of territory. Lot looked eastward, saw a charming, well-watered plain, and accordingly pitched his tent toward Sodom. Then came the battle of the kings, four against five, and Lot was taken prisoner. Either there was something particularly lovable about Lot, which appealed to Abraham, or it was merely the impelling force of blood-relationship; Abraham fought with the captors, and rescued Lot, his family, and his possessions. After this battle we have that mysterious and inexplicable picture of Melchizedek, a picture that torments one's curiosity:

And Melchizedek king of Salem brought forth bread and wine; and he was the priest of the most high God.
And he blessed him, and said, Blessed be Abram of the most high God, possessor of heaven and earth;
And blessed be the most high God, which hath delivered thine enemies into thy hand. And he gave him tithes of all.

There is one reference to Melchizedek in the Psalms, and eight in the letter to the Hebrews, but I doubt if the writer of the letter knew anything about him. He was, however, obsessed by the mysterious man, saying of him in the seventh chapter of Hebrews, "without father, without mother, without descent, having neither beginning of days, nor end of life, but made like unto the Son of God; abideth a priest continually."

The King of Sodom offered to let Abraham keep the captured goods provided he would hand over Lot and his family, which request was refused. Then Abraham's affection for Lot was still further shown when, after he had entertained three angels, who gave him a strong hint as to the immediate future of the city of Sodom, he pleaded with the Lord to spare the city. There is something humorously Oriental about Abraham's bargaining with Jehovah. Just as accuracy in statement is a modern virtue, so a fixed price in selling is both recent and Occidental. No trader in the East expects his first price to be the final one, nor does the buyer expect his original offer to be accepted. They are never in a hurry under the sun; both seller and purchaser rejoice in the artistry of bargaining and stretch it out as long as possible. Each understands the other's simulated frankness. So when Abraham first begged Jehovah to spare the doomed town, if it contained fifty righteous persons, and finally beat the number down to ten—the bottom figure—he showed himself a man of his time.

Two angels visited Sodom at even, and were entertained by Lot. On that night, the last night in the history of the city, the inhabitants completely demonstrated their fitness for damnation.

After the evil dark came a terrible dawn. Lot lingered, for he had warned his sons-in-law of the imminent disaster, and although they had sneered at him he may have hoped that at the last moment they would start. But he could not wait. Just before sunrise the angels took Lot, his wife, and two daughters by the hand and told them to escape to the mountain. To the disordered mind of the fugitive the mountain seemed almost as bad as brimstone, and he prayed that he might enter a tiny town close at hand:

Behold now, this city is near to flee unto, and it is a little one: Oh, let me escape thither (is it not a little one?) and my soul shall live.

This request was granted, and the city was thereafter called Zoar, which means "little." Lot entered this refuge just after sunrise:

The sun was risen upon the earth when Lot entered into Zoar.
And the Lord rained upon Sodom and upon Gomorrah brimstone and fire from the Lord out of heaven...
But his wife looked back from behind him, and she became a pillar of salt.

I have much sympathy for her. Lot lost some of his property, but she lost her home. A home means so much more to a woman than to a man that it is easy to understand why she looked back. Lot was thinking of his safety, but she was thinking of her house, and all the pretty things in it—all the furniture, all the ornaments, all the family china— burning up. Although her feet were carrying her away from the sulphurous flames, she looked back to what she loved, even as Orpheus looked back to his most precious treasure, coming out of hell.

There are many interesting men and women in the book of Genesis, and four great personalities: Abraham, Isaac, Jacob, Joseph. Abraham is a magnificent ancestor. Unlike most Old Testament heroes, hardly anything evil can be charged against him. He lied twice when the truth would have been practically as well as morally an improvement; but everything else he said and did is admirable. He came out of a pagan country, Ur of the Chaldees; his father Terah started with his son Abram, his daughter-in-law Sarai, Abram's wife, his grandson Lot, from Ur to settle in Canaan; but on their way they stopped at Haran; and Terah died in Haran.

Abraham was a spiritually minded man; he seemed to be in communication with God. He was invariably obedient to the divine voice, no matter what inconvenience or suffering resulted; for he had an unfaltering trust, which was rewarded. To signify his success as an ancestor his name was changed from Abram to Abraham. Abram means *father of height,* but Abraham means *father of a multitude.* His wife's name was changed from Sarai, which means *Jehovah is prince,* to Sarah, which means *princess.*

Abraham and Sarah are two of the very few characters in the Bible of whom it is recorded that they burst out laughing. There is almost no laughter in the Bible, except the mocking laughter of destiny; yet laughter was regarded as good, and promised to those who lived righteously. Both husband and wife were amused by the same promise— that they should have a son. Abraham was shaken by uncontrollable mirth, so that he rolled on the ground in merriment. Can't you see him holding his sides, and then unable to stand up?

Then Abraham fell upon his face, and laughed, and said in his heart, Shall a child be born unto him that is an hundred years old? and shall Sarah, that is ninety years old, bear?

Then as if to say, "Don't let's talk nonsense, let's keep to the facts," he cried to God, "O that Ishmael might live before thee!"

Evidently in a very few generations, longevity had come near to what we regard as normalcy; Abraham's ancestors apparently had children at what we should call a very advanced age.

The Associated Press reported that on 6 July, 1922, John Shell died in

Kentucky at the age of 134, and that he left two sons, one ninety and the other seven years old!

Sarah was about ten years younger than her husband, and also laughed at the idea, but in a more contained manner, as became a lady; yet when her son was born, she said with fine spirit, "God hath made me to laugh, so that all that hear will laugh with me." And the child was named Isaac, which means *laughter*.

The Arabs regard Ishmael as their ancestor; if is rather remarkable that Abraham's two sons, Isaac and Ishmael, should be respectively the fathers of the Hebrews and of the Mohammedans.

I do not share the common opinion that Abraham did wrong in offering up his son Isaac. On the contrary it is one of the most splendid of all his recorded deeds. The twenty-second chapter of Genesis gives this story with such brevity and simplicity that the effect is startlingly dramatic. There are to-day many conscientious objectors; they say that Abraham's obedience to God is fine, but when he was asked to give the life of his own son, he would have shown more nobility and righteousness had he flatly refused. Indeed, there are Christian divines who have found it hard to swallow this story, and it is plain they wish it had never been written. Yet men in our day not only consider it right to give the lives of their sons for what they regard as a higher call, but are universally honoured for doing so. What would be the general opinion of a man who, during the years 1914-18, had said, "No; I love my son too much to sacrifice his life at his country's command; it cannot be right for a father to give up his own son." Millions of parents followed Abraham's example, and gave their sons in response to what they believed was the call of duty. Nor did they feel any shame; they felt exalted. "I have two sons at the front!" And those who carried gold stars were assigned the place of honour in public celebrations. Do you remember Lincoln's wonderful letter to the woman who had sacrificed five sons for her country?

The attacks on Abraham's character are based on a lack of faith in God. He really believed in God, just as nowadays every man believes in his own country. If it be not only right but glorious to give one's son for one's country, so it was right for Abraham to sacrifice his son when the divine voice called.

To-day, in public addresses and public documents, God receives a complimentary vote; but when it comes to making a real sacrifice for Him the lack of actual faith is often painfully apparent. Men and women are proud of having sons at the front in time of war; but if they really believe in God they ought to be just as proud of having them away as foreign missionaries, in time of peace. Are they? Indeed, the supreme example of divine sacrifice is in the words, "God so loved the world that He gave His only-begotten Son." We give our sons for our country; according to the Gospel, He gave His for the contemptible world. Some persons have said ironically that many men will die to save others, and that if they had the chance to save the world by dying, anybody would do it. They rather miss the point: the sacrifice mentioned in the Gospel is as if a man should give his life to save a hill of ants.

Let us not condemn Abraham till we have begun to understand human nature in the twentieth century; for Abraham did exactly what millions of fathers have done in our day.

As the mediæval Mystery Plays interjected slapstick farce when they represented the comedy, *Noah's Flood,* so they added an original and more poignant note in the tragedy of *Abraham and Isaac.* They knew well enough that the love of mother and son is universal and elemental. Now the Bible says nothing of Sarah's feelings at the proposed sacrifice, nor of Isaac's thought of her in the supreme moment.

Attention is wholly centred on the father and son, as it is in Barrie's tragedy, *The New Word.* But in one of the old Mysteries we have a scene that must have produced a powerful effect, for it is impossible even now to read it coldly. Isaac becomes uneasy at the nonappearance of the animal for sacrifice, and asks his father some embarrassing questions. At first Abraham puts him off, but finally is forced to blurt out the truth.

A. Ah! Isaac, Isaac! I must kill thee!
I. Kill me, father? Alas! what have I done?
If I have trespassed against you aught,
With a rod you may make me full mild.
And with your sharp sword kill me not,
For surely, father, I am but a child.
A. I am full sorry, son, thy blood for to spill,
But truly, my child, I may not choose.
I. Now I would to God my mother were here on this hill!
She would kneel for me on both her knees to save my life.
And since my mother is not here,
I pray you, father, change your cheer,
   And kill me not with your knife.

Then Abraham explains that it is God's will and Isaac, while he cannot understand why God wishes him slain, submits.

I. Therefore do our Lord's bidding,
And when I am dead, then pray for me:
But, good father, tell ye my mother nothing,
Say that I am in another country dwelling.

Jews and Egyptians, Mohammedans and Christians, have usually buried dead bodies with care and ceremony; Hindoos burned them, and Parsees left them to be devoured. The first funeral mentioned in the Bible was that of Sarah, and for that purpose Abraham bought the first graveyard. Sarah died at the age of one hundred and twenty-seven, and after publicly mourning for her, Abraham bought of Ephron the cave of Machpelah, to be used as a family burying ground. The conversation between the two men has a modern flavour. Abraham offered to pay well for the place, and Ephron answered:

My lord, hearken unto me; the land is worth four hundred shekels of silver; what is that betwixt me and thee? bury therefore thy dead. And Abraham hearkened unto Ephron; and Abraham weighed to Ephron the silver, which he had named in the audience of the sons of Heth, four hundred shekels of silver, current money with the merchant.

Sarah was an interesting and charming woman and was mourned sincerely by both her husband and her son. When Isaac married Rebekah, we are told that "he was comforted after his mother's death."

Abraham lived to be one hundred and seventy-five, which was then regarded as old.

Then Abraham gave up the ghost, and died in a good old age, an old man, and full of years; and was gathered to his people.

Abraham had many other children, but Isaac and Ishmael, the sons of Sarah and Hagar, took charge of the funeral, and buried him by Sarah's side in the family lot. To his sons by other women Abraham had made gifts and sent them away; to Isaac he left his entire estate.

The unquestioning obedience that Isaac displayed when prepared for sacrifice by his father was symptomatic of his character; as a man, he seems to have lacked force and initiative. (What would have happened if Adam had tried to sacrifice Cain?) Isaac was a dreamy, romantic person, who accepted the wife his father provided for him, and then went under her thumb. He became a pathetic, childish, spoiled old man, over-fond of food, like many old people; and was easily bamboozled by his scoundrelly son Jacob. He was always in love with his wife, as we know by an amusing passage in the twenty-sixth chapter of Genesis. He lied to Abimelech, like his father before him, and said that Rebekah was his sister. Some time after, the good Abimelech looked out of a window and saw Isaac kissing Rebekah in a manner unusual between brothers and sisters. So here again a lie nearly brought disaster, where the truth would have been safer.

The courtship of Rebekah by the envoy sent by Abraham—who seems to have been a first-rate diplomat—is a pretty story. Rebekah at the well, with her pitcher on her shoulder, is a picture not easily forgotten. The messenger placed a gold ring in her nose. She ran into the house to show the presents given her by the stranger; and when her brother Laban saw those gifts he was impressed. We can see the greed in his eyes, for we know his later history. Perhaps Rebekah was glad to get away from him, for when asked if she would follow the ambassador home to marry a man she had never seen, she gave an unhesitating and unqualified affirmative:

And Isaac went out to meditate in the field at the eventide; and he lifted up his eyes, and saw, and behold, the camels were coming.
And Rebekah lifted up her eyes, and when she saw Isaac, she lighted off the camel.
For she had said unto the servant, What man is this that walketh in the field to meet us? And the servant had said, It is my master; therefore she took a vail, and covered herself.

This first courtship is told with much interesting detail, and is a true pastoral, unequalled in idyllic beauty until we come to the story of Ruth.

The twin sons of Jacob and Rebekah were the rufous Esau and the smooth Jacob; the former his father's and the latter his mother's favourite. Esau grew up to be a hunter and Jacob a "plain man dwelling in tents." The thick-headed, downright, impetuous fellow was no match for his crafty brother, who had learned sharp dealing in business. Although Jacob was blessed by God and became the father of the twelve tribes of Israel, it is impossible to admire him, or to forgive him for his treatment of his unsuspecting brother. When Jacob *sod*—boiled—pottage, it is probable that he knew what he was about, for the distinguishing characteristic of this young man was foresight. Esau came in from hunting with a hunter's appetite; and the smell of the cooking was too much for him, as Jacob had expected. So when he asked for food he found he had to pay his birthright for it. This privilege seemed to him an empty honour in comparison with eating; and like many other men, he sacrificed the future for an immediate and material good. The author of the letter to the Hebrews condemned Esau for selling his birthright; but from our point of view Jacob is more to be condemned for buying it. He was the first and one of the most contemptible in the long list of food profiteers.

But when Rebekah and Jacob—two of a kind— went into partnership to swindle both Isaac and Esau, the result was even more disastrous; the twenty-seventh chapter of Genesis, in its dramatic narration of this outrage, must be regarded, from the artistic point of view, as one of the finest short stories in literature. Nor is it the only instance where a mother and son have united to get something out of the father of the house.

It is interesting to observe that the authors of the books in the Bible seldom attempt to shield their heroes, or to palliate their offences. We shall see later, when we come to study the lives of the kings, that an extraordinary feature of the biographies is their lack of the nationalistic bias; and so, at the very outset of the history of the Israelites, the duplicity and treachery and selfishness of the father of the twelve tribes are set down with amazing candour. Love of truth triumphed over partisan feeling; which is one reason why the stories in the Bible make such interesting reading. Human nature as it really is arouses the interest of persons in all ages and in all countries; whereas plaster saints are dull. They are dull, not because people dislike goodness, but because the average man never likes to see men and women represented as untrue to human nature. There is only one perfect character in the Bible, and He was divine.

The worst service that can possibly be performed for a historical figure is for his biographer to represent him as perfect; readers lose interest in him. This is well brought out by Lytton Strachey, in his Life of Queen Victoria, where he accounts for the lack of interest among English people in the Prince Consort, who was really a man of extraordinary power, by the fact that the official biographies made him a pattern of all the virtues instead of a human being. No such error is committed by Bible authors; which is one reason why the men and women in the Bible are so vivid. It is a continual Revelation of Man.

Jacob had a well-founded fear that Esau would kill him; he fled to the stock farm of his uncle Laban, and there married two of his first cousins. On the way thither he had a vivid dream:

And he lighted upon a certain place, and tarried there all night, because the sun was set; and he took of the stones of that place, and put them for his pillows, and lay down in that place to sleep.
And he dreamed, and behold a ladder set up on the earth, and the top of it reached to heaven; and behold the angels of God ascending and descending on it....
And Jacob awaked out of his sleep, and he said, Surely the Lord is in this place; and I knew it not.
And he was afraid, and said, How dreadful is this place! this is none other but the house of God, and this is the gate of heaven.
And Jacob rose up early in the morning and took the stone that he had put for his pillows, and set it up for a pillar, and poured oil upon the top of it.
And he called the name of that place Bethel. (*House of God.*)

When Sarah Flower wrote her hymn, *Nearer My God to Thee,* which she and her sister sang as a duet in church, she was inspired by this particular incident in the life of Jacob.

Or, like the wanderer,
   The sun gone down,
Darkness be over me,

My rest a stone;
Yet in my dreams I'd be
Nearer, my God, to thee,
   Nearer to thee!

There let the way appear
   Steps unto heaven;
All that thou sendest me
   In mercy given;
Angels to beckon me
Nearer, my God, to thee,
   Nearer to thee!

Then with my waking thoughts,
Bright with thy praise,
Out of my stony griefs,
   Bethel I'll raise;
So by my woes to be
Nearer, my God, to thee,
   Nearer to thee!

The best part of Jacob's nature and the best thing in his life was his love for Rachel. He was a lover, and fell in love at first sight:

And while he yet spake with them, Rachel came with her father's sheep; for she kept them.
And it came to pass, when Jacob saw Rachel the daughter of Laban his mother's brother, and the sheep of Laban his mother's brother, that Jacob went near and rolled the stone from the well's mouth, and watered the flock of Laban his mother's brother.
And Jacob kissed Rachel, and lifted up his voice, and wept.
And Laban had two daughters: the name of the elder was Leah, and the name of the younger was Rachel.
Leah was tender-eyed; but Rachel was beautiful and well-favoured.

I used to think that this passage meant that Leah, although inferior in beauty to her younger sister, had lovely expressive eyes. Not at all; it means that Leah was sore-eyed. Poor Leah!

And Jacob loved Rachel; and said, I will serve thee seven years for Rachel thy younger daughter....
And Jacob served seven years for Rachel; and they seemed unto him but a few days, for the love he had to her.

When Jacob offered to serve seven years for Rachel, it was a high compliment to her worth. In Methuselah's time seven years were not very much, but later they were a goodly portion of a man's life.

Since the beginning of human history it has been sport to see the engineer hoist with his own petard; and it is not altogether with regret that we see the scoundrel Laban cheating his nephew, the scoundrel Jacob. They were an accomplished pair of robbers —diamond cut diamond, and Laban met his match. Jacob did not forget the trick Laban played on him. At the end of seven years rheumy-eyed Leah was worked off on him instead of Rachel; her father probably believing that this was the only way he could get his eldest daughter married, and at the same time he could keep Jacob another seven years. Jacob was a good workman, was plainly mad about Rachel, and would not go without her. So Jacob served another seven years for the woman he loved. Leah had more sons, but Rachel was the mother of Joseph, and subsequently died in child birth—the child was Benjamin. *Sed duo leones.*

Jacob swindled Laban neatly with the cattle, getting the strong ones for himself, and leaving the weaker ones for Laban; so he paid him back for the extra seven years. When Jacob, his two wives and children, decided to leave Laban, Rachel stole all the ikons out of her father's house; what was he doing with those household gods, anyhow? And what did Rachel mean to do with these graven images? She wanted them so badly that she lied about them to her father when he came after them, completely deceiving him.

The situation is similar to the elopement of Jessica with Lorenzo, for we know that when Jessica left her father's house she took something away with her. In *Merchant of Venice,* Shylock tells the whole story of how Jacob cheated Laban out of the cattle, not knowing that he would shortly be in the position of Laban, minus his daughter and the gold.

One night Jacob wrestled with an angel until the break of day, refusing to let go until he had received a blessing. He had his name changed by the angel from Jacob *(supplanter)* to Israel *(Striver with God),* and limped away tired but satisfied. Jacob never let go of anything until he had secured some personal profit out of it.

Every change in government, every advance in human history, has to be accomplished through human agency, imperfect, ignorant, and selfish as the means may be. It is not altogether surprising, therefore, that Jacob, whose character was spotted as his cattle, should have been selected as the father of the twelve tribes; he had ability, extraordinary tenacity, and was physically and intellectually fitted to be the head of a great race. His love of bargaining was so consuming that he would bargain with God Himself.

Joseph is the best man in Genesis, and one of the best men in history. He combined the romantic, dreamy nature of his grandfather with the practical ability of his father. He had none of Isaac's weakness, and none of his father's duplicity; or rather his father's selfish trickery changed into wholesome shrewdness in Joseph. He was not the last example of an upright son coming from a rascally father; there are many of them alive.

Jealousy in families began with the first; and as Cain hated Abel, Joseph's brothers hated him. He was only seventeen, his father's favourite, and he wore a conspicuously beautiful coat, that did not add to his popularity; when he told about his dream, where his brothers' sheaves made obeisance to his, they hated him yet the more. It is all natural enough, and given the same circumstances the same thing today would happen in Nebraska or Colorado.

Joseph went out to meet his brothers in the pasture; they saw him coming and their first plan was to kill him. But Reuben, the eldest, counselled that they put the boy in a pit, because he hoped to save him and bring him home to his father again; so they took off his coat and threw him in the pit. In Reuben's temporary absence the Ishmaelites came along with their camels, and Judah suggested that they sell Joseph to this caravan. We may discover here a kind of poetic justice, the son of Sarah sold to the son of Hagar, whom Sarah had treated with such fierce cruelty and jealous anger. The travellers carried Joseph off to Egypt. When Reuben returned, to his horror Joseph was not in the pit; and he rent his clothes.

And he returned unto his brethren, and said, The child is not; and I, whither shall I go? (What will become of me?)

Jacob really never recovered from the blow when his sons returned with Joseph's bloody coat. He refused to be comforted. There must have been many times when his brothers wished the boy were home again.

Joseph was like the industrious apprentice, and rose rapidly in favour in the land of Egypt; he was handsome, had excellent manners, was intelligent and reliable—one in a thousand. Captain Potiphar made him his overseer, and Potiphar's wife naturally fell in love with the young man and tempted him. But Joseph was loyal to his employer, and the rebuffed woman's feelings turned (once more naturally) into rage; she told her husband that Joseph had made advances to her, and accordingly Joseph was put in prison.

Observe that not only was Joseph man enough not to betray his benefactor, but he was man enough not to betray the woman; he knew it would break up the home, ruin his master's happiness, and cause the death of Potiphar's wife; so he chose to go to prison, having with him the consciousness of innocence. His character shone bright in the darkness of the dungeon and he was made a Trusty.

He interpreted the dreams of the butler and the baker. I have always been sorry for the poor baker, for there seems to have been no reason, except bad luck, why he should have had such a horrible fate, while the butler was taken back into high favour. It was simply a trick of destiny. Human nature comes out clearly in the butler; Joseph, after doing him a kindness, asked him to remember when he was in power again. "Yet did not the chief butler remember Joseph, but forgat him." Even so.

Two years later Pharaoh had a dream, which seems easy to interpret, though it baffled the magicians; his butler finally remembered the young Hebrew, and Joseph not only interpreted the dream, but became ruler of the land of Egypt under the monarch; he drove in a chariot, and people bowed the knee before him. He was thirty years old; it being thirteen years since he was sold by his brothers.

In the time of famine he had the position that was in recent years so successfully filled by Mr. Herbert Hoover; he controlled the food supply, displaying executive ability of the highest order.

The story of Joseph and his brethren is one of the greatest stories in the world; one of the most beautiful and most dramatic; as a revelation of the deep instincts of family affection, universally appealing. For every man, woman, and child in the world understands this emotion, however untrue they may be to its call or however often it may be silenced by the lust of money or the pride of life. Few things are more depressing than to see brothers fighting over their father's will.

Joseph talked with his ten brothers through an interpreter, and they naturally did not recognise in the prime minister their kin, yet the dream then came true, for they bowed down and did obeisance before him. They were required to return home, and fetch Benjamin; on the way Reuben reminded the others of their cruelty to Joseph in the old days, and how he had told them it would lead to no good. This was the only pleasure Reuben had on the melancholy journey. What Jacob's feelings were when he saw them returning without Simeon, who had been kept as a hostage, we do not know; but they were nothing to his despair when informed that Benjamin was to accompany them on the second expedition.

The orator of the family was Judah; it was his pleading that finally persuaded the old man to part with Benjamin, and it was Judah's masterly speech before Joseph that annihilated the barriers between them. It would have softened the heart of a sterner listener than he. Joseph broke down and wept aloud. There is no recognition scene in Greek drama finer than this.

The story is complete as it stands; but how I wish little Benjamin had spoken! When Joseph first saw him—"Is this your younger brother? God be gracious unto thee, my son."

Now I would give much to know what Benjamin replied to this greeting. But Joseph could not wait to hear; looking on the face of his brother, whom he loved more than the whole world, he knew his feelings would betray him. He hastily left the room, and wept in solitude.

When old Jacob was brought before Pharaoh, we cannot restrain a feeling of pity for the wretched old man, who all his life long had experienced prosperity without happiness. The Emperor asked him, "How old art thou?" and he replied:

The days of the years of my pilgrimage are an hundred and thirty years; few and evil have the days of the years of my life been.

After giving a separate blessing to each of his twelve sons—in which the supremacy of Judah is distinctly foretold—and to the two sons of Joseph, Jacob died, and at his own request was buried in the family lot, in the cave of Machpelah, where reposed Abraham, Sarah, Isaac, Rebekah, and Leah. But when Joseph died his embalmed body was placed in a coffin in Egypt, the home of his triumph, glory and final happiness. Later his bones were carried out of Egypt and buried in the Promised Land.

III

MOSES

A Great Man—His Meekness—Life in Egypt—His Failure as a Public Speaker—The Ten Plagues—The Events in the Wilderness—Laws and Law-Courts— Jethro—The Ten Commandments—The Calf of Gold —Death of Moses.

Just as in the American Revolution and again in the Civil War there appeared a Leader of genius, without whose wisdom, patience and unselfishness the result might in each case have been quite other than fortunate, so in the critical period of early Israelitish history—the residence in Egypt and the wanderings in the wilderness—there rose from the ranks a leader, law-giver and stateman—Moses. He must be called a great man. His public acts and private character are alike admirable. In addition to the books written about him by theologians and Bible students, he has been the subject of secular examination. Forty years ago I heard a lecture delivered by Henry George on "Moses, the Great Hebrew Statesman," and in 1920 a book was published by a scientific man, called "Moses the Physician," praising his learning, his foresight, and especially his belief in cleanliness and segregation of disease.

A famous parenthesis in the twelfth chapter of Numbers tells something definite about his character : "Now the man Moses was very meek, above all the men which were upon the face of the earth." This passage has damaged the prestige of Moses with modern readers; Moses, "the meekest man," has seemed a milksop. For although many persons are in reality mild and timid, they like to be thought of as bold, aggressive, and fierce. The difficulty here is in the word "meek," which in 1611 had a nobler connotation than in later times. It then meant gentle in manner, modest, and above all self-controlled, the crown of courage and strength. Meekness was the finest attribute of warriors and kings. When Chaucer made his picture of the Knight, a first-class fighting man, the hero of many wars, he added this touch:

And though that he were worthy, he was wys,
And of his port as meek as is a mayde.

He nevere yet no vileinye ne sayde
In al his lyf, unto no maner wight.
He was a verray parfit gentil knight.

Both in the Psalms and in the Gospels we are told that the meek shall inherit the earth. It has been said cynically that this is indeed the only way by which the meek could get it. Yes, but how about the violent and predatory? What success have they had? Consider Alexander, Napoleon, and the German Emperor Wilhelm II. They were rather the opposite of meek. They tried to control the earth, with what result is history. There is in reality no strength like the strength of meekness. That Moses was the meekest man in ancient history is the best thing said about him.

"I am meek and lowly in heart," is a portion of the autobiography of the only Person who ever overcame the world.

Like many great statesmen, Moses was not a fine public speaker. We are apt to believe that oratory is the main qualification for public life; whereas wisdom, foresight, and courage are superior to rhetorical gifts. Daniel Webster was a supreme illustration of the combination of mental and oral powers; but much of the most important work in statesmanship is done in committees, and by men who cannot make an impressive public address. I suppose Benjamin Franklin was the greatest committee man in history; one of the ablest American constructive statesman of our time, Herbert Hoover, is not an effective orator. President Hayes gave the United States one of the best administrations we have had; he also was no speech-maker. On his feet Grover Cleveland was dull, but he had the wit to know it.

At the outset of his career, Moses said unto the Lord: "O my Lord, I am not eloquent, neither heretofore, nor since thou hast spoken unto thy servant; but I am slow of speech, and of a slow tongue." ("I am so bad an orator that I cannot talk effectively even when divinely inspired.") That which is the very breath of life to many politicians, public speaking, was always a terror to Moses; there was nothing he hated more. Like almost all men, Moses failed as an after-dinner speaker, as we learn from his lack of success immediately after the fall of manna.

Aaron, the Levite, was selected to do the talking; he was inferior to Moses, both in intelligence and in character; "he shall be to thee instead of a mouth, and thou shalt be to him instead of God." Moses was to tell Aaron what to say, and Aaron was to say it with emphasis and elegance. This worked well; but when Aaron, in the absence of Moses, relied on his own ideas, the result was disaster.

Perhaps Moses would have produced a more speedy effect on the hard heart of King Pharaoh, if he had had the gift of public speaking. It was all Pharaoh could do to listen to him, and the royal personage was not impressed. But Moses held the trumps, as his adversary eventually discovered.

Labour troubles began in Egypt, as they have begun in some other countries, by oppression. The good king, Joseph's friend, was dead; and one of his successors on the throne took a familiar and natural, though erroneous, policy toward the numerous and powerful aliens in the land. He looked about him and saw that the Israelites were many in number and successful in business; that is, they were adding to the wealth and prosperity of the country. (Most natives have never been able to endure this.) Had the king dealt kindly with the Jews, there is no saying what might have been the greatness of Egypt and the glory of the ruler; but human nature cannot be expected to show the wisdom of gentleness and the conquering power of good will. Pharaoh said to his courtiers, "Come on, let us deal wisely with them." (Now the wisdom of this world is foolishness with God.) "Therefore they did set over them taskmasters to afflict them with their burdens."

The service increased in rigour and cruelty, and the workers grew ever more numerous and strong; so the policy of extermination was decided upon; instead of changing the medicine, he increased the dose. But it is difficult to subdue human beings by severity, and the Irsaelites found a way to escape extinction. Then a man and wife, both of the house of Levi, had a handsome boy; his mother hid him in the reeds by the river. When Pharaoh's daughter looked into the basket, the baby began to cry; about the only time in his life when his eloquence had an immediate effect; it should be remembered that his audience was composed of women. By a neat device, his own mother was hired as nurse; the child grew up under her care, and under the protection of the Princess. Pharaoh's daughter not only saved him, but gave him his name Moses, which means *Drawer Out;* and she said, "Because I drew him out of the water." She named him better than she knew; for he drew the children of Israel out of slavery. She was a good girl, and I wish we knew more about her.

We are ignorant of the facts of Moses's childhood and adolescence. His first recorded act as a man was harshly resolute, and prophetic of his future powers of deliverance. He saw an Egyptian beating up a Hebrew, and he killed the tormentor. But the next day he saw two of his own people fighting; and endeavouring to restrain them, he spoke to the aggressor, who insulted him by asking him if he meant to murder, as he had murdered the Egyptian. This was the first of a long succession of insults that Moses was to receive from his countrymen.

Moses fled, entered the land of Midian, and there married one of the seven daughters of Jethro. This man Jethro, being grateful for "meek" Moses's services in standing up alone for his daughters against a whole pack of roughs, treated him kindly. It is interesting to notice that Moses unconsciously prepared himself for the position of leader of the nation by living the quiet, reflective life of a shepherd, which was later David's occupation before becoming a king.

It was while Moses was keeping the flocks of his father-in-law, that he experienced the first of many divine revelations, and knew that he had been selected as the inspired leader. He saw a flame of fire in the midst of a bush, and yet the bush was not consumed. Moses turned to look at it out of curiosity; but when he heard the voice calling to him from the flame, and answered, "Here!" like a boy at school, he was told to come no nearer. Then he hid his face, for he was afraid to look upon God. After receiving his commission, he rather boldly enquired, What name shall I use in speaking of the Divine Voice?

To this question he received a reply that shows how profoundly spiritual the religion of the Israelites was, and how superior to all their contemporaries they were in their conception not only of One God, but of that. God as Pure Spirit. Compare this not only with the paganism and polytheism so common in the world, but with such a familiar and childish notion as *le bon Dieu;* where half the people use the expression naively, and the other half with condescending contempt. Moses was told to say unto the children of Israel that I AM had sent him. No modern philosophy has been able to define the Supreme Reality with more accuracy, brevity and dignity. With God it is always the present tense; man is quickly in the past.

Moses, like most of his race, was not easily convinced even by God; and he knew that the people would be sceptical of his story unless he could prove it. So he was allowed to perform a variety of miracles; his rod turned into a snake, his hand became leprous and whole again, and greater works were promised.

Pharaoh, like other kings, did one good thing; he died. It is extremely fortunate for the good of the world that kings have shared this peculiarity with their subjects; it is probable that Death has done much toward making the world safe for democracy. To be sure, a new Pharaoh appeared, who was no improvement; but that particular one could torment the world no longer.

Moses and Aaron went in to interview the king, but it is plain that he regarded them as dangerous radicals, labour-agitators; so far from listening to them, he tried the method subsequently adopted by Rehoboam and by many rulers in more recent times. He attempted to crush their spirit by increased severity, a plan which has many ardent advocates in all epochs, though history seems to prove its inadequacy. "Let there more work be laid upon the men, that they may labour therein; and let them not regard vain words." ("I'll show them!")

Thus the brilliant scheme was adopted of having the Israelites make bricks without straw, which brought about so acute a crisis in the labour situation that it will never be forgotten. I remember being a listener to a debate in the House of Commons in 1900, when a Conservative, who was conspicuously lacking in talent, attempted to make a speech amidst the heckling of the turbulent Irish members; he was describing work on some public building, and he proceeded as far as the unfortunate word "bricks"; instantly the Irishmen roared out as though the chorus had been carefully rehearsed: "Bricks without straw!" and the speech was buried in derisive laughter.

If Abraham was the father of the children of Israel, Pharaoh was the father of the Bourbons. He learned nothing and forgot nothing. He called in his magicians and had them attempt to rival the enchantments of Moses and Aaron; this is the first time the competitive method appears, which later was to be used with such success by the prophet Elijah. The spectacle interested the royal observer, but it hardened his heart against Moses. It now became necessary to make a demonstration that should affect the whole Egyptian people; and we have the dramatic series called the Ten Plagues— a tragedy in ten acts, ending with a climax. The horrible events came in this order:

I. Blood.	VI. Boils and Blains.
II. Frogs.	VII. Thunder and Hail.
III. Lice.	VIII. Locusts.
IV. Flies.	IX. Darkness.
V. Murrain.	X. Death of the Firstborn.

Aaron stretched out his rod: the water in the Nile turned into blood, as well as every pond, pool, and creek; even the waters in the kitchen pans became blood, and an intolerable stench arose from dead fish. This lasted seven days; and the magicians, trying their technique, found that they could turn water into blood just as easily as their rivals. Their real prowess would have been better proved if they had reversed the process; as it was, they merely added to the general discomfort. Pharaoh was no more affected by the blood than if he had been Louis XV. Kings have seldom been afraid of blood; and nothing on earth is more stubborn than your true reactionary. Then came millions of frogs; the Egyptian magicians, apparently pleased with this miracle, tried their enchantments and found that they could increase the population of frogs, though there seem to have been plenty without their assistance. But the king did not like frogs, and he sent for Moses and Aaron. It appears to me that the stupidity of this monarch reached its climax in the answer he made to the question put by Moses; the Hebrew asked: "When shall I make supplication that the frogs return to the river?" The king answered: "Tomorrow." If he had had rudimentary common sense, he would have said, *Today; this minute.*

Next day the frogs died just where they were; and for a time they were more potent dead than alive. But no more came; and Pharaoh refused to let the Hebrews go. Then came lice, billions of them; they covered every man and beast in Egypt. Pharaoh paid no attention to them; he may have noticed nothing unusual.

The magicians, who had been conspicuously successful with the frogs, tried to create lice; but here they failed and were then convinced that Moses and Aaron were inspired. Their professional admiration for their competitors, in whom they now recognised masters in their own art, was so great that it exceeded their fear of the king; they told him what they thought about the situation, but Pharaoh would not listen.

Then came the flies; it was unendurable; Pharaoh spoke to Moses, who abolished the plague; immediately the king was himself again. Then came murrain, a pestilence which destroyed all the cattle; Pharaoh was interested sufficiently to make enquiries as to the extent of the disease; but he remained firm. Then came boils, which later were to try the patience of Job, but the king would not relent. Then there was a frightful storm, thunder and lightning and hail, which wrought untold damage to man, beast, and crops. Pharaoh could not endure it, and he said quaintly: "I have sinned this time." The storm ceased, carrying Pharaoh's repentance with it. There came a fresh east wind, bringing numberless locusts, which ate up everything that the hail had spared, so that the farms looked as if recently visited by the army worm. Pharaoh had another attack of remorse; the west wind came and blew the accursed locusts into the Red Sea, so that there was not one left in the whole country.

A friend writes me: "I wonder do you know of the locust plague in Jerusalem, during the war? The locusts came 'out of the clear sky,' suddenly. They ate every vegetable thing except wood, stripping a tree to its bare twigs and branches within an hour. The government ordered everyone to bring in his peck or so of dead insects each day. The poor earned their living, collecting the daily quota for others. Tin is the best offensive. The American colony's special technique was to 'shoo' the insects along converging, low, tin-walled canals into sunken gasolene tins. But this seemed like trying to empty the ocean with a medicine dropper. Finally, when no green thing is left, the plague passes on, abruptly. And no one knows whither the locusts go, as no one knew whence they came."

The plague of locusts was followed by Egyptian darkness, thick darkness for three days, so that no man could see and no man dared move. Pharaoh sent for Moses, and when the darkness was lifted and the pleasant light returned, he said bitterly to the man of God:

Get thee from me, take heed to thyself, see my face no more; for in that day thou seest my face thou shalt die.

And Moses said, Thou hast spoken well, I will see thy face again no more.

Then came the last terrible plague, the killing of the firstborn in the night, and the first passover, when the Lord passed over the favoured people; an event that is still annually and solemnly celebrated by millions.

There arose a great cry in Egypt; both the king and the people besought the aliens to depart. In the midst of this turmoil, there is one touch of humour. The children of Israel "borrowed" of the Egyptians jewels of silver, and jewels of gold, and raiment.

They had been in Egypt four hundred and thirty years when the great exodus began; and then they were not allowed to take the short way to the Promised Land through the country of the Philistines, but were led south-east to the Red Sea. In front was the Pillar of Cloud by day and the Pillar of Fire by night.

Pharaoh ought to have been glad to see the last of them; but either he regretted his defeat or the loss of the borrowed jewels; he pursued them with chariots and horsemen; so the Israelites, who preferred life to honour and slavery to death, bitterly attacked Moses and for the first time raised a protest that was to be heard more than once: "We were better off in Egypt."

But the Red Sea opened; the timid and querulous multitude passed through in safety. Then in the darkest hour before the dawn the waters returned and swallowed up the Egyptian host, soldiers, chariots, and horsemen. And in the morning light the children of Israel saw the pleasantest sight their eyes had ever beheld.

"Israel saw the Egyptians dead upon the sea shore."

I remember hearing Phillips Brooks preach a notable sermon on that text. We may have sorrows in the future; we may have enemies tomorrow; but there are difficulties, there are evils that we survive. They can never annoy us again. "Israel saw the Egyptians dead upon the sea shore."

The immediate troubles of the Hebrews were over; the troubles of Moses began. He had more vexations with his own people than he had had with his avowed enemies. Human nature asserted itself in the wilderness. In spite of their great deliverance and the mighty evidence of God's favour and of the inspiration of Moses, the people were constantly discontented; they were always on the point of rebellion. The genius for complaining, which is inherently human, found almost daily expression; until the patience of Moses was exhausted.

The shortest distance from Egypt to the Promised Land is considerably less than the distance from Philadelphia to New York; so far as miles were concerned, Canaan could have been reached in a week. But Israel was not fit to occupy Canaan or indeed any other country, as the behaviour in the wilderness abundantly proved. The famous Elizabethan "atheist," Marlowe, said that Moses was a miserable leader, because it took him forty years to lead his people a short distance; he could have done much better himself. These forty years in the wilderness, however, were necessary; and never did a leader and statesman show finer capacity for meeting both chronic and acute difficulties.

Furthermore, during these wanderings a complete system of laws, both moral and technical, became established; the health of the people was cared for by a definite set of hygienic regulations; the ritual for worship was proclaimed. The Israelites reached Canaan when, and not before, they were mentally and physically fit to settle there.

It was perhaps natural that in comparison with the privations and hardships of the wilderness, Egypt looked good; they saw it only in retrospect and, as is frequently the case, the difficulties of the past faded out of the picture, and they remembered only their homes and their regular meals, as indeed a free man will sometimes during a vacation spent in voluntary camping. They complained of the lack of food, so manna rained down from heaven. It covered the ground like a frost, was white to the eye and sweet to the taste. When the people complained of thirst and nearly mobbed Moses, he was divinely ordered to strike a rock, and pure water gushed out. These are some of the chief events that were recorded during the journey.

One day, Jethro, Moses's father-in-law, appeared on the scene, bringing the wife of Moses and their two sons. On the next day, Moses took his regular place as a judge, and began to hear complaints and cases of all kinds, both little and big. The petitioners had to stand in line for hours, and justice was almost as slow as it is now. Jethro watched the proceedings awhile, and then told Moses that all this would wear both him and the nation out; he advised that Moses select a number of able and upright judges, who could settle relatively unimportant cases, while Moses should be the Supreme Court. This admirable counsel was followed; and so the children of Israel not only had a set of laws and ordinances, but a court system to administer them. Then the good Jethro departed into his own land, and we see his face no more. So far as I know, there is no further allusion to him in the Bible. But he ought not to be forgotten.

The laws established by Moses were fair and reasonable, and in all that concerned man's dealing with man were adapted to the times and the people. They often went beyond mere scrupulosity, and enjoined kindness to strangers, gentleness to widows and orphans, and consideration for animals. The nineteenth chapter of Leviticus contains rules that ought to be remembered to the eternal honour of their maker. People were forbidden to reap the *corners* of their farms; gleanings must be left for the poor and the stranger. Labourers must be paid at the end of the day's work; "the wages of him that is hired shall not abide with thee all night until the morning." Cruel practical jokes were forbidden; no doubt some boys thought such things were funny. "Thou shalt not curse the deaf" (I have heard American boys do this) "nor put a stumbling-block before the blind." Rich and poor were to be treated exactly alike in court. "Thou shalt not go up and down as a tale-bearer." Courtesy and etiquette were taught by law. "Thou shalt rise up before the hoary head, and honour the face of the old man." They must see to it that they have just balances and just weights.

Those who maintain that the Mosaic Law was harsh and cruel should remember that the following verses are in Leviticus, though many seem to have forgotten the fact:

Thou shalt not hate thy brother in thine heart.
Thou shalt not avenge, nor bear any grudge against the children of thy people, but thou shalt love thy neighbour as thyself.

When Our Lord gave the eleventh and twelfth commandments, he was quoting from Moses, as He was when He said: "I will give you rest."

The presence of laws forbidding many strange sins and crimes seems to indicate that so-called unnatural evils were known to exist there and then, as they have in all nations since.

There was the same fondness for superstition and the same eagerness to be gulled as there is today. "Regard not them that have familiar spirits, neither seek after wizards."

The Ten Commandments, which have had such a prodigious influence in human history, are all prohibitions except one. The chief sins are forbidden in the Tables of the Law, and it would be difficult indeed to have arranged at that time a list of regulations that would have covered a wider area of human conduct with fewer words.

Clouds and darkness surrounded Mount Sinai at the giving of the Fundamental Law.

There were thunders and lightnings, and a thick cloud upon the mount, and the voice of the trumpet exceeding loud; so that all the people that was in the camp trembled.

And Moses brought forth the people out of the camp to meet with God; and they stood at the nether part of the mount.

And Sinai was altogether on a smoke, because the Lord descended upon it in fire; and the smoke thereof ascended as the smoke of a furnace, and the whole mount quaked greatly.

And when the voice of the trumpet sounded long, and waxed louder and louder, Moses spake, and God answered him by a voice.

Although many in the audience forgot to keep these commandments, it is certain that no one forgot the day and the manner of their announcing.

I. *Thou shall have no other gods before me.*

In the ancient world, man was polytheistic; here was the promulgation of one Divine Principle. Literally translated, it reads: "You shall have no gods except me." More and more, this commandment is seen to be the expression of philosophical truth. Later, the children of Israel ran after other gods with tragic consequences; and in the twentieth century, the German Empire broke the first commandment, worshipping the gods of iron and steel as revealed to man in huge armaments. This is now a common form of paganism, perhaps the most popular religion in the world, numbering more adherents than all other systems; yet it is an illusion, for there is only one God.

And just as nations have madly worshipped other gods, so individuals have constantly substituted other gods for the Ideal; the gods of money, of influence, of pleasure, of social position, of fame; most common of all and most tragically absurd is the substitution for the Eternal Spirit of Truth and Right—One's Own Self.

II. *Thou shalt not make unto thee any graven image . . . for I, the Lord thy God, am a jealous God, visiting the iniquity of the fathers upon the children unto the third and fourth generation of them that hate me; and showing mercy unto thousands of them that love me, and keep my commandments.*

This and the Fourth are the longest of the commandments, containing respectively ninety-one and ninety-four words. It was necessary to forbid idol-worship, to which the Israelites continually surrendered, copying, as so many nations do, only the evil features of their rivals; remember how Rachel, Jacob's wife, stole the images out of her father's house, and how bitterly ironical was the language of the prophet Isaiah in dealing with this form of superstition. The awful words, "I am a jealous God," give offence to many people today, but they are a statement of simple fact. Religion is the most jealous thing in the world, more jealous than any woman. There is only one place in the human heart for religion—the first place. It must have that or nothing. It must either dominate a man's life, be the supreme, controlling factor, or it becomes as ornamental as a graven image, and as powerless. Those who use religion as a decoration, or as a last resort in fear and sickness, betray their real paganism in brushing it aside when their personal, selfish interests are concerned. Religion is never content with a weekly contribution, or a large occasional present, or a tribute of courtesy; religion demands the heart, the inmost citadel; and unless it has that, it wants nothing. Either religion is the most vital of all truths, or else it stands for silly superstition, and should not be allowed to annoy and harass conduct, any more than Napoleon permitted it to interfere with his purposes. He went as far as anyone has gone without religion, and he is perhaps more to be admired than those who wish to have it both ways, like a man who gives presents to his wife, and his heart to some one else.

The last part of this commandment, which speaks of the remote consequences of evil-doing (and also, be it remembered, of virtue) particularly enrages the enemies of religion. Thomas Hardy sneered at it in *Tess of the D'Urbervilles*, saying it might be good enough for Divinity, but was scorned by average human nature. Precisely so; it is scorned by average human nature, which is one reason why there are so many unfit children born into the world. Their lifelong weakness and suffering come from the selfishness of their ancestors, who scorned this commandment, just as they scorned the established truths of science, of which this is a powerful affirmation. The second commandment will be supported by every family physician, and by students of society like Henrik Ibsen.

III. *Thou shall not take the name of the Lord thy God in vain.*

Never was this commandment more needed than in the twentieth century. Swearing is instinctive in human nature; all men are naturally cursers, but that does not make them admirable. There has been an enormous increase in swearing within recent years. Of all habits, it is the most difficult to break.

IV. *Remember the Sabbath Day to keep it holy.*

Six days shall thou labour, and do all thy work.

An old divine wisely pointed out the fact that there was more profanation of the second sentence than of the first. "Six days shalt thou labour." If this commandment were universally followed, there would be enough food, fuel and clothing for everyone in the world. Every lazy, idle, and useless person breaks the fourth commandment six times oftener than other men. The first clause means: "Remember the day of rest and keep it inviolate." Take one day in seven off, provided you have earned it; don't let anything interfere. It is curious that so many persons have thought it more wicked to have recreation on Sunday than to work. Sunday was never meant to be a day of gloom; it ought to be the happiest day in the week, for God blessed it. The ideal use of that holiday is to devote it to religion and recreation; forget business and the regular round of toil. Experience seems to show that people need one day in seven; the French Revolutionists tried to make it one day in ten, but the experiment was not successful. An excellent way to spend the day is to go to church and thank God in the morning, and enjoy some outdoor sport in the afternoon. The Sabbath was established for man's health and happiness, as our Lord pointed out.

V. *Honour thy father and thy mother: that thy days may be long upon the land which the Lord thy God glveth thee.*

It is often called "the only commandment with promise," but those who say so forget the Second. That length of days should be associated with filial affection seems curious; for some cruel sons have lived long. But, more closely examined, it is not longevity, but continued residence on the family property that the statement emphasises. Affection and care for one's parents keep up the estate; neglect of them means wandering, and the invasion of strangers. It is unfortunate that parents love their children so much more intensely than children love their parents; but the whirligig of time brings in his revenges. There is no commandment that parents must love their children, for the commandments were in every instance directed at common sins.

VI. *Thou shalt not kill.*

Do no murder. Some extremists have held that this means one should not kill a quail or a woodcock. Nonsense; but it is true that as we grow older, we more and more appreciate the gift of life and hate to take it away. Few young people think shooting is wrong; but there are plenty of conscientious objectors among adults, Thomas Hardy, for example, and Emerson, who said: "Hast thou named all the birds without a gun?" A little common sense is useful here, as elsewhere; the wanton destruction of animals is no doubt wicked; but if it be wrong to go out and shoot an occasional partridge, then it is even more wrong to kill chickens. For you feed chickens and pretend that you are interested in their welfare, when in reality you are a traitor. The wickedness in shooting enormous bags of game, raised for the purpose, consists in the fact that many wounded ones escape, and while you are eating your dinner and talking merrily of a "good day's sport," these wretched creatures are in agony.

VII. *Thou shalt not commit adultery.*

Every adulterer is also a liar and usually a sneak. It is interesting to observe that many men who would not lie to others in business, will break their word given in the church before many witnesses. The reason is largely a matter of cowardice. If a man breaks his word to another man, penalties follow, whereas a man can break his word to a woman with impunity. But adultery is founded on falsehood and dishonour fully as much as corrupt dealing in trade. In the fifth chapter of Numbers, there is a strange but impressive method of dealing with jealousy and adultery.

VIII. *Thou shall not steal.*

Which ought to apply as much to embezzlement and crooked manipulations as to house-breaking or borrowing apples.

IX. *Thou shall not bear false witness against thy neighbour.*

Which refers, I suppose, not merely to perjury, but to slander and malicious gossip.

X. *Thou shall not covet.*

Observe that all of these commandments are meant to preserve from harm those who accept them, not merely those who might be victims. It is not pleasant to have a thief steal from you, but it is much better for you than to steal something yourself; it is unfortunate to be killed, but it is better than to go out and kill somebody. That is, the commandments were not only necessary for the welfare of society, but fidelity to them is necessary for individual happiness. The tenth is wholly devoted to this purpose; it does not hurt your neighbour if you covet his house; some persons are so constituted that this adds to their delight; but it hurts *you* horribly and poisons your peace of mind. I suppose covetousness of one's neighbour's possessions drives more people into financial difficulties than any other vice.

The twentieth chapter of Exodus, containing the Ten Commandments, which might be called the Moral Constitution, is immediately followed by a succession of chapters, which might be called the By-laws, because they give specific regulations. Then follow detailed directions for the ritual of worship; very tedious reading this is today, but doubtless important then, in order that the people might have ever before them the thought of Divine Leadership.

Human nature lost little time in asserting itself; despite the wonders they had seen, despite the terrible majesty of the promulgation of the Law, what do we hear of the people's behaviour? Well, they did exactly what millions are doing today; they forsook the worship of God for the worship of the Golden Calf. Moses could not trust the people out of his sight; they behaved like bad boys in the absence of the teacher. Moses was away in the mount; and the children of Israel said to Aaron: "Up, make us gods, which shall go before us; for as for this Moses, the man that brought us up out of the land of Egypt, we wot not what is become of him." To the eternal discredit of Aaron, he surrendered to mob sentiment at just the moment when a strong voice was most necessary. Apparently the women had much jewelry, perhaps the finery they had "borrowed" from the Egyptians; Aaron fashioned the whole collection into the form of a golden calf and worshipped it with song and dance.

Imagine the feelings of Moses coming down the mountain with the two tables of the Law, his mind still in the solemn obsession of the Divine Presence. That honest young lieutenant, Joshua, hearing the racket below, said to Moses: "There is a noise of war in the camp." Moses replied crisply: "It is not the voice of them that shout for mastery, neither is it the voice of them that cry for being overcome; but the noise of them that sing do I hear."

He made up his mind that they would shortly sing another tune. When he saw the calf and the idiotic dancing around it, ungovernable rage possessed him; he smashed the tables he was holding. When a man is in a state of terrific rage, he simply has to smash something or burst; it is an immense relief to take it out of the furniture.

The rest of this narrative is downright funny. Moses took the golden calf, burnt it, powdered the ashes, made a soup of it, and forced the whole congregation to drink it! If you want your calf, down with it. Then Aaron behaved even worse than Adam in Eden; in response to the sharp questions of Moses, he said: "You know these people; they are always bent on mischief." Then he declared that he had taken their golden contribution. "So they gave it to me; then I cast it into the fire, and there came out this calf." Was there ever a more ridiculous, a more childish lie? Can't you see the liar's face?

Observe that meek Moses was not rebuked by God for smashing the tables; he was given new ones in their place. He was punished for only one thing — because he had momentarily lost confidence in God at the waters of Meribah, when he was more afraid of popular clamour than of God Himself. For this reason he was not permitted to enter the Promised Land.

Moses lived to be one hundred and twenty years old, in sound bodily and mental health. His eye was not dim, nor his natural force abated. His farewell charge to the people is filled with poetry and splendid imagery, containing many promises and many warnings. Like all persons, they needed advice, received it, and forgot it. Human nature is revealed in their shortness of memory; for nothing is more frequently heard than good advice, and there is nothing so quickly forgotten. The first alluring picture is enough to drive it out of the mind.

One passage in this farewell speech retains its flavour: "Thou shalt lend unto many nations, and thou shalt not borrow."

Moses stood on Pisgah Heights, on Mount Nebo, and looked with what emotion we can only imagine on the fair panorama of Canaan. He could not enter it any more than Abraham Lincoln could live to see the growth of the mighty nation he had saved. But Moses, though he had little confidence in the people, knew that their immediate future was assured; that the results of his wisdom and foresight would last long; he saw the travail of his soul and was satisfied.

IV

FAMOUS FIGHTERS IN CANAAN

Wilderness Tragedies—Nadab and Abihu—Korak and the Earthquake—the Spies—Horrors of War—Rahab—Fall of Jericho—Achan—Death of Joshua—Defeat of Sisera—Gideon and the Desperado Abimelech—Story of Jephthah—Samson and His Exploits— Tragedy in the Tribe of Benjamin.

There were terrible adventures in the wilderness; for there was treason in high places, and it was punished in spectacular style. The sons of Aaron— Nadab and Abihu—so eloquently mentioned by Browning in *One Word More*—together with their father and Moses and seventy elders, went up the mountain and saw the glory of God.

And they saw the God of Israel; and there was under his feet as it were a paved work of a sapphire stone, and as it were the body of heaven in his clearness.

Yet later Nadab and Abihu, who had seen the King in His beauty, offered up strange fire near Sinai, and instantly perished. So quickly forgotten then and now is the Divine Revelation; forgotten by those especially chosen to receive it.

Miriam, the Prophetess, sister of Moses and Aaron, may perhaps be pardoned for family jealousy when Moses married a black girl, an Ethiopian; but her method of revenge was strange, and the punishment accurately fitted the crime. Together with Aaron she started a sedition and was smitten with leprosy; as much as to say, If you think you are better than your sister-in-law because you are white, you shall be even whiter by contrast, white as snow. The leprosy was removed at the entreaty of Moses, but it gave Miriam something to think about.

Korah, a Levite, with two hundred and fifty princes, men of renown, started an open rebellion against Moses. The latter felt this defection in the priest tribe, and he said sharply: "Ye take too much upon you, ye sons of Levi." The next day, in the presence of the whole congregation Moses called upon the people to keep away from Korah and his friends; there was an instant and dramatic separation, as if Korah had some horrible and contagious disease, and the doomed men stood out in appalling loneliness.

And it came to pass, as he had made an end of speaking all these words, that the ground clave asunder that was under them: And the earth opened her mouth, and swallowed them up, and their houses, and all the men that appertained unto Korah, and all their goods. They, and all that appertained to them, went down alive into the pit, and the earth closed upon them; and they perished from among the congregation. And all Israel that were round about them fled at the cry of them; for they said, Lest the earth swallow us up also.

The shrieks of the sinking rebels must have rung in the people's ears for many days; yet they were soon ready to rebel and to worship other gods, which is the way of all flesh. The famous story of Balaam and his ass would seem to indicate that in spiritual insight a donkey may have more intelligence than a man.

There were also frightful plagues, devastating pestilences, one of which carried off fourteen thousand and seven hundred; there was the scene of the serpent in the wilderness. Yet these wonders made no permanent impression, for the children of Israel, like those of other nations, were more interested in their food than in their souls, Moses needed all his meekness, all his self-control, to deal with them.

Spies were sent out into the Promised Land, and with the exception of two stout-hearted men, Joshua and Caleb, they brought back an evil report. They said:

It is a land that eateth up the inhabitants thereof; and all the people that we saw in it are men of a great stature.
And there we saw the giants, the sons of Anak, which come of the giants; and we were in our own sight as grasshoppers, and so we were in their sight.

The time came, however, to advance; and from now on the history of Israel is like the history of other countries, a succession of wars. The progress of the world has been made through bloodshed, wholesale slaughter, with innumerable and unspeakable individual cruelties. The triumphs of Israel are no exception; they came at the expense of their antagonists and through their own losses. Children were brutally murdered and captive women became the spoil of the Chosen People. The Promised Land was won; a land flowing with milk before the Israelites appeared; then the milk turned to rivers of blood. War was what it always has been; crops and property were destroyed, babies butchered, greed and sensuality were unrestrained. The soldiers of Israel were "thorough" and carried out the policy of extermination amid the braying of trumpets and psalms of thanksgiving. So far back as we can trace events since Adam, man has lived under a curse.

There was really nothing exceptional in the fate of Damocles; in the midst of our feasting the sword is ever over us, suspended by a single thread.

As Moses was a statesman, Joshua was a soldier. His predominant qualities were strength and courage. He was an invader by divine right. Still on the east of the Jordan, he sent out two spies to enter the first important city near the other bank, the city of Jericho. They went into the house of Rahab, a harlot; women of this profession were known in the beginning of history, for mention is made of them in the book of Genesis. Rahab had the two men on the roof of her house, and covered them with the stalks of flax; when the king of Jericho enquired for them she put the messengers on a false scent. Rahab had heard the story of the drying up of the Red Sea, and the conquests of the men of Israel; she believed in them with all her heart; she knew that the doom of Jericho was at hand. She begged for the life of her family, was told to mark the window of her house with a bit of red, and keep everybody indoors; then the house and the inmates would be spared. Such marking of friendly houses was common in the recent war.

Her house was on the town wall, and she let the spies down from the outside window by a cord; they escaped to the mountain, hid there three days, and returned in safety to Joshua.

Thus Rahab acquired immortality; she is mentioned with respect in the Letter to the Hebrews and in the Letter of James. She has frequently appeared in imaginative literature. In our time women of her profession are often idealised, and made the heroines of fiction and drama. There are writers who seem to have a sentimental admiration for people of this class.

The children of Israel passed through the river of Jordan, following the ark of the Lord. The method was slightly different from that in which they had crossed the Red Sea. There they passed between two walls of water; here on one side the water was amassed in a heap, and on the other it ran off entirely and disappeared. Perhaps the only person who was not surprised by the event was Rahab; she remembered the story of the Red Sea and knew that for the Israelites a stretch of water was no obstacle.

Shortly after they had arrived in safety on the Canaan side, a curious thing happened; the fall of manna ceased and has never been seen since. They were now to have a table prepared for them in the presence of their enemies.

Joshua had a vision of a strange captain who came to meet him, which is not surprising, as many in the recent war saw plainly similar apparitions.

The gates of Jericho were closed. Six days in succession the Hebrew men-at-arms walked once entirely around the town, preceded by seven priests carrying in silence trumpets of rams' horns, followed by the Ark of God, which in turn had a rear-guard; as the inhabitants looked from the walls at the grim and silent host they must have felt extremely nervous. On the seventh day the invaders circumvented the city seven times—presumably at the double-quick—and then the priests blew a tremendous blast, the army gave a mighty shout, and down went the walls! With the exception of Rahab and her family, every living thing in the city was slain by the Israelites, and Jericho wiped off the map of Canaan.

The soldiers were told to take no booty for themselves, but one man, Achan, found his avarice stronger than his fear of the mighty God; he hid valuables in his tent. Then came a terrifying casting of lots. The twelve tribes were drawn, and Judah was taken. What a relief for the others, and what consternation in the heart of Achan! The families of Judah were drawn, and the Zarhites were taken; man by man they were drawn, and Zabdi was taken; his household was drawn, and his grandson Achan was taken.

And Joshua said unto Achan, My son, give, I pray thee, glory to the Lord God of Israel, and make confession unto him; and tell me now what thou hast done; hide it not from me.

Achan confessed. He and his entire family were stoned and then burned. A great heap of stones was raised over him to commemorate his sin and its punishment. The heap was still there when the chronicler wrote his narrative.

The Canaanites did not yield up their fair land without a struggle; they were brave in battle, like soldiers everywhere, and they fought desperately, but they had no more chance than Hector against Achilles. Their hour had struck. The familiar military tactics appear, strategy and ambush; and there were traitors who espoused the Hebrew cause, some of whom were kept indefinitely as hewers of wood and drawers of water. The sun stood still over Gibeon, stood still in the midst of the heaven, and set only with the fortunes of the town. Then comes a touch worthy of Marlowe's *Tamburlaine*. Five kings had hid in a cave; when they were brought out, Joshua called forward his captains and told them to put their feet on the necks of the kings. After this indignity the five were slain and hanged on five trees, which had never borne such royal fruit before.

So the invaders went on their way, houghing horses, destroying armed hosts, butchering women and children and burning cities; the pillar of fire and pillar of smoke were now of their own making, and marked their progress continually. Finally the land was divided up and perforce submitted to the peace of victory.

Here and there the Canaanites made those bloodless conquests that subdued nations often win of their conquerors; some of the Israelites adopted the gods of their foes, and others made marriages with the daughters of the land. So it has ever been.

The time came for Joshua to die. He made an impressive farewell speech, full of warnings against transgression, full of promises to the faithful, and he said, "Behold, this day I am going the way of all the earth." The brave old warrior, who, like Cromwell, carried the law in one hand and the sword in the other, made a covenant with his people and submitted to death with a calm and steadfast mind.

After the death of Joshua the people became corrupted by following the religion of their enemies; victories came to an end. Eglon, the king of the Moabites, got the upper hand and held Israel in subjection eighteen years. This led to the first political assassination recorded in the Bible. King Eglon was a very fat man, "and he was sitting in a summer parlour, which he had for himself alone." A revolutionist named Ehud entered, saying that he had a message from God. As the heavy monarch got up out of his chair, Ehud pushed a dagger into the nearest part of his anatomy, which stood out conspicuously; the fat closed over the handle, and Eglon fell. Ehud left the room quietly, closing and locking the door after him; the king's attendants, thinking he did not wish to be disturbed, left him alone long enough for Ehud to make good his escape and rouse his people. The Moabites were thoroughly beaten, and there came eighty years of peace. The Israelites attempted some loose form of general government, under judges, who are first mentioned in the second chapter of the book. It is interesting to note that women seemed to have full political equality, for one of the most famous judges was Deborah, who was a poet as well as a statesman, and who celebrated the treacherous murder of Captain Sisera by a splendid battle-hymn:

The inhabitants of the villages ceased, they ceased in Israel, until that I Deborah arose, that I arose a mother in Israel......
Awake, awake, Deborah; awake, awake, utter a song; arise, Barak, and lead thy captivity captive, thou son of Abinoam.......
And the princes of Issachar were with Deborah......
For the divisions of Reuben there were great thoughts of heart.
Why abodest thou among the sheepfolds, to hear the bleatings of the flocks?
For the divisions of Reuben there were great searchings of heart.
They fought from heaven; the stars in their courses fought against Sisera.
The River of Kishon swept them away, that ancient river, the river Kishon. O my soul, thou hast trodden down strength.
Then were the horsehoofs broken by the means of the prans-ings, the pransings of their mighty ones......
Blessed above women shall Jael the wife of Heber the Kenite be, blessed shall she be above women in the tent.
He asked water, and she gave him milk; she brought forth butter in a lordly

dish......
The mother of Sisera looked out at a window, and cried through the lattice, Why is his chariot so long in coming? Why tarry the wheels of his chariots? Her wise ladies answered her, yea, she returned answer to herself,
Have they not sped? Have they not divided the prey; to every man a damsel or two; to Sisera a prey of divers colours, a prey of divers colours of needlework on both sides, meet for the necks of them that take the spoil?
So let all thine enemies perish, O Lord; but let them that love him be as the sun when he goeth forth in his might.

It is interesting to note that Sisera's mother was interested in fine needlework; she seems especially to have admired the skill of the Jewish women.

Forty years of rest followed the defeat of Sisera; then the Israelites made their accustomed deviation into idolatry, and the victorious Midianites ruled over them seven years. They were finally delivered by the cautious and sceptical Gideon, who must have tried God's patience with his doubtings, questionings and bargainings, but who for some reason was rewarded. His faith, like that of many others, depended wholly on facts and figures. I cannot regard him as a hero; he took no chances. For a considerable less display of doubt, Moses was forbidden to enter the Promised Land. The calculating shrewdness of human nature, the desire to invest only with assured profit, are sharply revealed in the character of Gideon.

The book of Judges abounds in brilliant short stories; the adventures of Gideon are thrilling, and those of that ruffian, his son Abimelech, even more so. This ambitious and reckless young man conspired against his brothers even as Edmund conspired against Edgar in *King Lear*. Instead of buying a birthright, like Jacob, he took it by audacity and force; for although he was conspicuously lacking in religion and morality, he never lacked courage. His creed was that of Napoleon—Might makes Right. Dominion and authority belong to those who are ready and willing to take advantage of opportunity. So at this point in Israel's history a conscienceless, melodramatic and picturesque daredevil appears on the scene and wins headship by a *coup d'état*. It is a stirring story, the story of Abimelech the Adventurer.

Gideon had seventy legitimate sons and also Abimelech, born of his maidservant in Shechem. When the father was dead Abimelech visited his own mother's relatives and put before them this question of government: Is it better to have seventy rulers or one? He drew them over; they gave him money, by which he secured a gang of hired cut-throats—"wherewith Abimelech hired vain and light persons, which followed him." He began his turbulent career by butchering his seventy brothers, with the exception of clever Jotham, who hid himself. Abimelech was then formally crowned king.

But Jotham, who was a persuasive orator, stood on an elevation, and, poised a-tiptoe for flight, he pronounced a sylvan allegory to the multitude, beginning authoritatively, for he felt himself to be the legitimate heir:

Hearken unto me, ye men of Shechem, that God may hearken unto you. The trees went forth on a time to anoint a king over them; and they said unto the olive tree, Reign thou over us.

But the olive tree said unto them, Should I leave my fatness, wherewith by me they honour God and man, and go to be promoted over the trees?
And the trees said to the fig tree, Come thou, and reign over us.
But the fig tree said unto them, Should I forsake my sweetness, and my good fruit, and go to be promoted over the trees?
And the trees said unto the vine, Come thou, and reign over us.
And the vine said unto them, Should I leave my wine, which cheereth God and man, and go to be promoted over the trees?

Apparently it was as hard to get good men to go into politics as it is now in America; and they refused for the same reason.

Then said all the trees unto the bramble, Come thou, and reign over us.
And the bramble said unto the trees, If in truth ye anoint me king over you, then come and put your trust in my shadow: and if not, let fire come out of the bramble, and devour the cedars of Lebanon......
If ye then have dealt truly and sincerely with Jerubbaal and with his house this day, then rejoice ye in Abimelech, and let him also rejoice in you:
But if not, let fire come out from Abimelech, and devour the men of Shechem, and the house of Millo; and let fire come out from the men of Shechem, and from the house of Millo, and devour Abimelech.

(Jerubbaal was another name for Gideon; Millo was a fort near Shechem; Shechem itself was an important town in sacred history, the first Canaan city visited by Abraham, the scene of the crowning of Abimelech, later of Rehoboam, and the place where Jesus spoke with the woman of Samaria.)

Jotham let this prophecy of civil war sink into the people like a poisoned arrow; it was a more powerful speech than if he had indulged in vituperation or jealous rage. And after three years there was dissension between Abimelech and his people; an agitator named Gaal, who lacked the courage of his convictions at the critical moment, induced the people to rise against Abimelech. That resolute man had no difficulty in defeating Gaal and the rebels, and took fierce vengeance on Shechem. A small party escaped and hid in a stronghold of the house of the god Berith. But Abimelech, who feared neither God nor man, adopted the same method that brought such terror to the heart of Macbeth. He and every man in the army carried a bough on their shoulders, and advanced like a moving forest; as they drew near to the place of refuge, they set fire to it, using their boughs as fuel; so was fulfilled literally and impressively the prophetic allegory of Jotham. In a subsequent fight, Abimelech had his skull cracked by a stone dropped from a woman's hands; and he commanded his armour-bearer to slay him, that he might not die in disgrace. He was consistently masculine; he died as he lived, by the sword.

Social inequalities, characteristic of all communities in time of peace, are annihilated by the common danger in time of war. As Abimelech, the son of a housemaid, had risen to be king, so Jephthah, the son of a harlot, who had been expelled from his father's house by his legitimate brothers, was sent for when Israel was attacked by the Ammonites. For in war the question is not, Who was your mother? but, What can you do? and Jephthah was a mighty man of valour. He was proud and clever enough to tell the ambassadors that if he agreed to lead them in battle they must acknowledge him as ruler after the victory. To this they agreed; and we see in the history of Israel, as elsewhere, how a powerful leader may rise from humble origin. Jephthah, like the wise man he was, tried to avoid open hostilities with the children of Ammon, and a spirited correspondence took place between him and their king; when negotiations failed, he smote them, hip and thigh. If only he had not made his famous vow!

Jephthah and his nameless daughter are immortal figures of tragedy; they conquer more people every day than Jephthah did on the happiest and saddest day of his life. She died for her country, and for her father's honour; every year thereafter the daughters of Israel celebrated her heroism with public lamentation.

Before her death she went upon the mountain with other young girls to bewail her virginity. Perhaps she showed more courage in this prolonged and solemn contemplation than if she had begged for instant sacrifice.

Just what she was bewailing I did not fully understand when I first read the story in my childhood, but I was impressed by it, and still more impressed by the sensation I caused in a room full of people one evening when I regarded my maiden aunt, who for some reason seemed to be depressed, and suddenly in a general silence I shot this question at her: "Are you bewailing your virginity?"

The Ephraimites, jealous of Jephthah's glory, and forgetting his grief, started a civil war against him, in spite of his attempts to remonstrate. Like a true statesman, he never resorted to war if it were possible to avoid it. Jephthah won the battle, which was the cause of another never-to-be-forgotten incident. The men of Gilead stood at the passages of the river Jordan, and when the fugitive Ephraimites came up, pretending to be of another tribe, and desiring permission to cross over, an interesting philological test was made.

... The men of Gilead said unto him, Art thou an Ephraimite? If he said, Nay;

Then said they unto him, Say now Shibboleth: and he said Sibboleth; for he could not frame to pronounce it right. Then they took him and slew him at the passages of Jordan: and there fell at that time of the Ephraimites forty and two thousand.

When one hears the English language to-day mispronounced, misaccented, and treated with vulgar carelessness by those natives who ought to respect it, one wishes there might be some public test and drastic penalty. "Sibboleth" for "Shibboleth" is surely no worse than "weat" for "wheat."

About twenty-five years after the death of Jeph-thah, the sinister shadow of the Philistines begins to spread across the Promised Land; it will be remembered their country stood directly in the path of the Israelites when they escaped from Egypt, and it was owing to this obstacle that the Hebrews made a wide detour. They inhabited a part of the sea-coast on the southwest portion of Canaan, though their army seems to have been much more important than their navy. The original hindrance was prophetic; they were to give Israel trouble many years; for the Israelites surrendered to the Philistine gods before surrendering to their men-at-arms. The Philistines had beaten and ruled the Hebrews forty years when Samson was born. He hated the foreigners as Hannibal hated Rome, and it was destined that he should trouble them.

An angel of the Lord appeared to Manoah and his wife, predicted that they would have a son, that he must be a Nazarite, and keep the vows; after which the angel ascended to heaven before their astonished eyes.

The word Nazarite means *Separated,* and the rules which a Nazarite must obey were set forth with precision in the sixth chapter of Numbers.

He shall separate himself from wine and strong drink, and shall drink no vinegar of wine, or vinegar of strong drink, neither shall he drink any liquor of grapes, nor eat moist grapes, or dried.
All the days of his separation shall he eat nothing that is made of the vine tree, from the kernels even to the husk.
All the days of the vow of his separation there shall no razor come upon his head.....he shall be holy, and shall let the locks of the hair of his head grow.

You see he was forbidden even grape juice; and he must neither shave nor have his hair trimmed.

Samson is the champion athlete of the Bible and, like most athletes, was then and is now enormously popular. College undergraduates are often ridiculed for their worship of football players; but they are merely following afar off the manner of the world. Men who are physically powerful have ten times more admirers than those who are intellectually distinguished; this fact is more evident to-day than in the age of the cave man. Never have prize-fighters been more popular than now. Samson has always been an appealing figure. Although ideally unfitted for the position, he was appointed Judge, and judged Israel for twenty years. Like most heavyweight athletes, he was a good fellow and good-naturedly generous when not opposed; but he was not conspicuous for intellectual brilliancy; his head was as solid as the muscles on his arms. He was fond of betting and an easy prey to women; his humour expressed itself in practical jokes. He never had his hair cut but once, and found that even more expensive than it is to-day.

Like most stupid people, he took the easiest way and followed his instincts. He saw a Philistine girl and wanted to marry her; in response to the expostulations of his father, he merely replied: "Get her for me; for she pleaseth me well."

It is interesting to notice that this Philistine foreign wife betrayed him to the Philistines; prophetic of the later conduct of Delilah. Samson paid his bet in grim fashion, and then left his wife to herself. It is characteristic of him, however, that he came back to her, his desire always being stronger than his wit; and when he found his "best man" had taken her, he destroyed the harvest of the Philistines with illuminated fox tails. His method of destruction showed more originality than the results thereof; for on a subsequent occasion he slew a thousand Philistines with the jawbone of a certain animal, which is by no means the last illustration of what widespread havoc can be wrought by an ass.

Another woman nearly proved his destruction; and he would have been lost if he had not had the unusual advantage of being able to walk out of the locked gates of the city, taking them with him as he went. Delilah finally succeeded in compassing his downfall; she did it not by cleverness, but by persistently being herself. I remember as a boy, Samson's giving her his secret seemed to me inexplicable; how could he be such a fool? He not only knew the necessity of keeping his strength, but her absolute treachery had been proved in his presence three times. My father had found it impossible to explain the situation to me, though I noticed it seemed natural enough to him. One must have lived some time in the world in order to understand how natural it was; it happens every day. Samson was not the only fool in the world.

It was not until he became blind that he really saw the truth. Good health often blunts one's perceptions. Do you remember the infinitely melancholy words of Gloucester, when in response to a sympathetic enquiry, he said:

I have no way, and therefore want no eyes:
I stumbled when I saw.

Either Delilah did not tell the Philistines the reason of his weakness, or they were stupid enough to forget it; they should have kept the prison barber at him every day. I suppose, however, they enjoyed watching his feats of strength, which they made him perform in public for their amusement; he willingly acquiesced in satisfying their curiosity, knowing that it was necessary to keep in condition.

Milton made a glorious poem out of Samson's sufferings. He understood them. He, too, had suffered both by blindness and women. Milton never forgot his first wife, and in the colloquy between the captive giant and Delilah, who had the assurance to visit him, there is more than a touch of autobiography.

After the Philistines came general anarchy; no king had as yet been appointed, and no judge had succeeded Samson. "Every man did that which was right in his own eyes," which means they all did wrong.

A quarrel over one woman started a terrific civil war, which nearly annihilated the tribe of Benjamin. This horrible story, a duplicate of what happened in Sodom, illustrates the unnatural wickedness in Israel, and the sacredness of hospitality, according to which the safety of a guest was considered more important than the welfare of the family. The tale is told with Russian intensity; and the battle that followed the death of the woman is set forth in detail. The children of Benjamin, who were on the defensive, had a number of sharpshooters.

Among all this people there were seven hundred chosen men lefthanded; every one could sling stones at an hair breadth, and not miss.

The city of Benjamin was taken by a stratagem; much slaughter resulted. Now the other tribes had all taken a vow that not one of them would give his daughter to a man of Benjamin in marriage. Later, their hearts softened toward the outcast tribe, and the method by which—while still the vow was kept inviolate—the surviving warriors of Benjamin secured wives is rude, violent, and decidedly interesting.

V

RUTH, ELI, SAMUEL, JONATHAN, AND KING SAUL

A Beautiful Short Story—A Hebrew Pastoral—Character of Ruth—Her Steady Loyalty—Sorrows of Naomi—Mothers and Daughters—The Mature and Prosperous Boaz—His Relations With His Farmhands—His Kindness to Ruth—Her Subtle Flattery— Her Choice of a Husband—Land-contracts—Ruth the Great-grandmother of David—Eli and His Sons—The Training of Children—The Younger Generation— Death of Eli—The Ark of God—Ichabod—Boyhood of Samuel—His Character—Saul the Cowboy—His Appearance—The First King—His Love of Music— His Prophesying—Degeneration of Saul—Fighting the Philistines—Character and Exploits of Jonathan—Saul a Constitutional Monarch—Display of Public Sentiment—The Death of Agag—Incorruptibility of Judge Samuel—The Ghost, the Medium, the Prophecy— Suicide of Saul—Reflections on His Character and That of Kings in General.

Ruth is a pretty name: in Hebrew it means *friendship* and in English *pity*. She lived up to her name in both languages; she was both loyal and sympathetic. She is one of the most attractive girls in the Bible; her gentle, affectionate nature seems all the fairer in contrast with two terrible women of the Old Testament, Delilah and Jezebel. A charming oasis is her story—one of the best short stories in literature—coming as it does between two long books of crime and slaughter.

There is nothing sentimental and nothing insipid in this idyl; it is a suburban pastoral, illustrating the grace of loyalty. We have learned in the twentieth century not to minimise the virtue of loyalty; this fine flower of human nature has its roots deep in the human heart. The beauty of loyalty consists in giving rather than receiving; giving all if need be, and asking nothing before or after. Selfish and calculating persons are conspicuously without it; and it is not fully understood by men of pure intellect. But there is always something splendid, something refreshing, about people who have it. You remember in

Shakespeare, when the various nobles were disputing as to whether the king had a legal claim or not, the strong voice of Clifford is like a breath of fresh air:

King Henry, be thy title right or wrong,
Lord Clifford vows to fight in thy defence.

One of the reasons why the character of D'Artagnan is so irresistibly attractive is because Loyalty was his religion; the whole man rings true, said Stevenson, like a good sovereign.

Naomi had reached the darkest hour of her life; driven from her country by famine, she migrated with her husband and her two sons. In the alien land of Moab, her husband and then both her sons died, leaving her a solitary Israelite, bereft of kin and fortune. She started to return home, and advised her two Moabite daughters-in-law not to accompany her; they were both young, and could marry again among their own people. Orpah kissed her, but Ruth clave unto her, and spoke out those words that have brought down the ages their eternal fragrance, as fresh and sweet to-day as when first uttered:

Whither thou goest, I will go; and where thou lodgest, I will lodge; thy people shall be my people, and thy God my God:

Where thou diest, will I die, and there will I be buried: the Lord do so to me, and more also, if ought but death part thee and me.

There are women who, like Lady Macbeth, are meant to bring forth men-children only, but they are perhaps not the most fortunate. The relation of mother and daughter is peculiarly beautiful; each needs the other so keenly, and they understand each other, because they are both women. A woman may be proud of her son, but she can never be so close to him as to her daughter. The neighbours were right when they said to Naomi, Ruth "is better to thee than seven sons."

Boaz was like a prosperous American farmer, head of a vast estate. He was a sound, hearty, healthy man, broad-minded and generous, whose relations with his hired reapers were cordial. He came out of the city to the fields, greeted the farmhands affectionately, and they responded in like manner. Then he noticed the slender girl, bending over the sheaves of grain, and upon enquiry found it was that very same foreigner of whose devotion to Naomi he had heard. One can easily imagine how his first agreeable impression of her appearance was strengthened by his knowledge of her amiable and affectionate character. He spoke to her kindly, and then he said something to the young men that wins our hearts:

And let fall also some of the handfuls of purpose for her, and leave them, that she may glean them, and rebuke her not.

Boaz had reached the age when he was flattered by her evident liking for him, for he had supposed that he must henceforth be and remain Boaz-sit-by-the-fire.

Blessed be thou of the Lord, my daughter: for thou hast shewed more kindness in the latter end than at the beginning, inasmuch as thou followedst not young men, whether poor or rich.

The common opinion is that men select their wives. While this undoubtedly happens here and there, it is equally true that women select their husbands. Boaz was marked down from the start by both mother and daughter, and he literally had no chance of escape. Fortunately for him, he fell into good hands; for a damsel that had shown such single-hearted devotion to Naomi would be faithful and loyal to the man of her choice. That very expression which we use so often, "the man of her choice," is significant.

We have a pleasant glimpse here of business dealings and the manner in which land contracts were secured. The historian narrates as though the custom in his own time had become obsolete.

Now this was the manner in former time in Israel concerning redeeming and concerning changing, for to confirm all things; a man plucked off his shoe, and gave it to his neighbour: and this was a testimony in Israel. Therefore the kinsman said unto Boaz, Buy it for thee. So he drew off his shoe.

Ruth married an upright and successful business man; and Naomi went wild with delight at having a grandson. She "laid it in her bosom, and became nurse unto it." Her troubles were over. The boy was named Obed, and became the grandfather of a mighty king. The last word in the book of Ruth is *David*. "And Obed begat Jesse, and Jesse begat David."

After this bright episode, the familiar story of war and of apostasy returns; the clouds gather again. Old Eli is a pathetic figure. He judged Israel forty years, was sincere and upright, submissive to the will of God. But like many religious men, he was not successful in bringing up his sons; perhaps his tacit acceptance of things as they are— for he was a religious fatalist—made it difficult for him to impose his will on his two bad boys. He remonstrated with them, when what they needed was something more drastic. They were altogether too much for him, and their depravity bewildered as much as it shocked the old man. There was no point of contact, no mutual understanding between Eli and his children. He was as incomprehensible to them as they to him. This is a tragic but unfortunately a familiar spectacle in family life. Judging by the frequency with which the topic comes up in social conversation, in magazine articles, and on the stage, it is regarded as a particularly difficult problem in the year of grace 1922. Some children shock their parents, and some parents bore their children. There has always been a quarrel between the older and the younger generation, but since the World War the quarrel has passed into an acute stage. If it were not for the fact that the younger generation are dependent on their parents for a source of supplies, it seems that often they could get on very well alone. The advice of father to son is often the last word in futility; the advice of son to father is to the effect that he had better not meddle with what he does not understand.

It is only where piety in the parents is accompanied with tact, sympathy, and understanding, where the intelligence of the father and mother is respected by son and daughter, where the boy would really like to resemble his father and the girl her mother, that one sees an admirable family life; fortunately such examples are not extinct. Eli was dense. He could not make religion seem real to his sons. He went to church, and they went to the devil. At the very gates of the house of the Lord, they indulged in sensuality and crooked dealing. The Sabbath school was to them a means of flirtation and the offertory a means of support.

Eli was too placid, too good-natured, to have keen perception; his mind decayed with his eyes. He thought Hannah was drunk when she was praying; and in the charming scene when the Voice came to little Samuel in the night, old Eli was neither excited nor jealous at the divine preference. But his reverence for the ark of God was high and sincere; he was like some Church priest to whom the ritual of the Church and everything connected with formal worship are more holy than a broken and a contrite heart. When the fateful messenger came from the field of battle and his appalling tidings proceeded from general to particular—as is so often the tragic unfolding of news—the army is defeated, your sons are killed, the ark of God is taken, then Eli "fell from off the seat backward by the side of the gate, and his neck brake, and he died; for he was an old man, and heavy."

His son Phineas left a wife with child, near her time. Some idiot told her the news of the defeat and dishonour of Israel, and of the death of her husband and father-in-law. She travailed and died; and just before her death the women spoke to her cheerily, and said, "Fear not: for thou hast born a son." They spoke to deaf ears: "she answered not, neither did she regard it." But she had named the child Ichabod, which means *Where is the honour?* her last words being, "The glory is departed from Israel."

I wish we knew something about Ichabod; he is never mentioned again in the Bible except in the fourteenth chapter of I Samuel, where Ahitub is called Ichabod's brother. But although the Bible is silent about him, he has been borrowed many times in literature and in history for his symbolical name. Whittier applied the word to Daniel Webster in 1850, not realising that the speech for which that statesman was condemned was the finest and most patriotic utterance of his life.

The boy Samuel was dedicated by his mother Hannah to Jehovah's service; he became a great religious leader, never deviating from the path of sanctity and rectitude. Yet to me he is not a sympathetic figure; he had more holiness than charm. There is something unlovely about the man, something rigid and puritanical. I suppose it was natural, brought up as he was, that he should be a prig in youth and a statue of severity in old age. He had no more luck with his sons than Eli; they were bad, as perhaps might be expected, and did not find the piety of their father alluring. Just as some humanitarians are kind to everyone except members of their own family, so I suppose some religious leaders have more zeal for God's house than affection for their own. Samuel's sons, like those of Eli, were a public scandal.

Samuel's stern integrity made him a powerful Judge, respected and feared by the people, whose wanderings after strange gods he did not hesitate to condemn. He went on circuit through various cities, holding court. The Philistines were in terror of him, for so long as his decisions were regarded, the Israelites prospered in battle; the power of the enemy receded, not to become triumphant again until after his death. He made his sons judges; they were corrupt, taking bribes freely, and the old man was shamed in the courts of law. The Israelites may perhaps be pardoned for their wish to have a king; they knew Samuel could not last much longer and they regarded with natural apprehension the coming rule of his sons. They spoke to him with cruel frankness:

Behold, them art old, and thy sons walk not in thy ways: now make us a king to judge us like all the nations.

Samuel was angry, not for the first or the last time in his life; and he warned the people that their king would be a tyrant. But they, fearing his decrepitude and his sons' depravity, wanted a personable figure of a king, who should go before them, lead them into battle, and incarnate the power of the whole nation. Their request was granted; the first king of Israel was the biggest and handsomest man in the country, every inch a king.

The tallest man came out of the smallest tribe, the tribe of Benjamin. Kish was a mighty man, a rich cattle-dealer, and

he had a son, whose name was Saul, a choice young man, and a goodly: and there was not among the children of Israel a goodlier person than he: from his shoulders and upward he was higher than any of the people.

I suppose he stood about six feet nine in his sandals.

Saul was a cowboy; and he had gone out to seek his father's strayed cattle when he met Samuel, the Seer, the man of God. The venerable prophet gave him the astounding tidings that he was to be king. Saul was modest and unassuming; he reminded Samuel that he belonged to the smallest of the twelve tribes, and that his family were socially unimportant; but Samuel took the embarrassed young man into the parlour, and gave him the place of honour at a state dinner of thirty guests. That night a bed was made for Saul on the roof of the house—perhaps he was too big for the indoor furniture—and the next morning Samuel anointed him as the first King of Israel. A peaceful but permanent change took place in the government of the nation.

Samuel made a curious prediction which came to pass that day. As young Saul drew near to a hill, he met a company of prophets descending; they were following musicians who were playing on the psaltery, tabret, pipe and harp, while mystic speech filled the air; Saul was particularly affected by music; his spirit was caught up in a strange exaltation, and he too shouted in ecstasy and prophesied with the rest. When his former friends saw this, they marvelled. They were as much astonished as college students would be to see their champion athlete suddenly break out in poetry. Saul's utterances sounded like tall talk for a young cattle-man, and they wondered what was the matter with him. They expressed their quite natural amazement in words that have become a proverb:

What is this that has come unto the son of Kish? Is Saul also among the prophets?

Saul became his natural self after this experience, for when Samuel was on the point of introducing him to the people, and like a convention speaker was just about to mention the name of the candidate, Saul could not be found; his shyness had got the better of him, and he had hid himself. But when he was found and presented to the congregation, they were delighted with his magnificent appearance, and they shouted together:

GOD SAVE THE KING!

Samuel wrote out a constitution, placed it in a book of records, and dismissed the people.

It is always easy to adjust one's self to an advance in the scale of living; luxuries soon become a matter of course. The big country lad, so shy and modest at first, quickly became used to the pleasures of authority. It was a bad thing for Israel to have a king, but it was even worse for the king. We see the old, familiar, melancholy story of pride, egotism, and an abuse of power leading to degeneration and ruin. The personal history of Saul is one of the most tragic in the Bible. Like Macbeth, he was a good fellow ruined by promotion. When we first meet Saul, we see a kindly, modest, country boy of superb physique, contented with his work, and happy in his exuberant health and strength; as soon as he became king, he exchanged comfort for splendour, cheerfulness for majesty, outdoor life for councils of state, peace of mind for chronic anxiety.

Furthermore, his moral nature had never been tried, and it failed to meet the tests of kingship. As his royal power increased, the wholesomeness of his character diminished. Men are not made for unchecked dominion, and almost invariably deteriorate with supreme power in their hands. The instance of Napoleon is simply a revelation of human nature; one sees the degeneration of the man steadily and insidiously accompanying the increase in authority. There are not many characters in history like Abraham Lincoln; whereas Napoleon, minus genius, is such a familiar example, so true to form, that Emerson took him as the representative of the common man.

It is depressing to contemplate the wretched figure of King Saul talking with the ghost of Samuel, and to compare that colloquy with their first conversation. On this last fateful interview, the same thing had really happened to both men; Samuel was an actual ghost, but in reality no more so than Saul, for he was only the ghost of his former self.

The deterioration of any man or woman is a shocking spectacle; but how much more so when the individual has been entrusted with enormous power and unbounded opportunities, only to make a wreck, involving his final ruin in the general downfall. Saul's youth was like a sunny spring morning, that changes into the darkness of clouds and tempest. His fate hurts us, because there is something about him that we love.

The Philistines were not unlike later conquerors; after they had beaten Israel, they hoped to make their enemies permanently helpless, as so many victorious nations have vainly hoped. There was not a single blacksmith left among the Hebrews:

For the Philistines said, Lest the Hebrews make them swords and spears: But all the Israelites went down to the Philistines, to sharpen every man his share, and his coulter, and his axe, and his mattock...
So it came to pass in the day of battle, that there was neither sword nor spear found in the hand of any of the people that were with Saul and Jonathan: but with Saul and with Jonathan his son was there found.

Like Frederick II, King of Prussia, Saul was fond of tall soldiers, and chose a special company of them to be the royal bodyguard. He searched the whole nation for individual athletes; "and when Saul saw any strong man, or any valiant man, he took him unto him." This company of picked men-at-arms, every one splendid in figure and famous for deeds of prowess, must have made an imposing appearance as they followed the mighty king, majestic in stature, head and shoulders above them all. These were the good days of Saul's reign, when he wore golden opinions in their newest gloss.

One of the most splendid and lovable young men in the Bible is the crown prince Jonathan; he was mighty and valiant, bold as a lion, fearless in danger, a good son and good patriot, and so loyal to his friend David that he was willing to lose his own rights rather than have David suffer. He was a natural-born soldier, who fought with wisdom and courage, and who died on the field of battle.

The Philistines had left a garrison at Geba, and, as frequently happens, the alien soldiers had corrupted the natives. Young Jonathan went forth to war, and smote this garrison, revealing at the same time the apostasy and abominable practices of the Israelites there dwelling. The Philistine host came out from their country hot for revenge, and the Hebrews hid "in caves, and in thickets, and in rocks, and in high places, and in pits." While the unarmed population were in this state of terror and apprehension, Jonathan, without telling his father, took his armour-bearer, who seems to have been a youth after his own heart, loving adventure more than life, and the two, climbing up the face of the rock with their hands and feet, rushed upon the army, like a pair of hounds into a herd. They slew man after man.

Afar off, the watchmen of Saul observed the confusion in the enemy's ranks and reported it; Saul gave the word, the Israelites advanced, and all the people came out of their hiding-places and fell upon the Philistines, while the natives rose against the garrison; there was a terrific slaughter. But a curious thing happened, which is of deep significance, for it proved to Saul that he was a constitutional monarch, when he had fondly believed himself to be absolute and irresponsible. He had forbidden every man to eat until night came and their revenge should be complete. Naturally, Jonathan had not heard the king's command, and being almost faint with the heat of his exertions, and seeing honey in a wood, he ate of it; the relief he felt could not have been better expressed than by the Bible phrase: "His eyes were enlightened." Then the people, in horror, told him of his father's words, but the sensible Jonathan declared his father to be in error, and that it would have been better for all the people to eat, and so be more efficient in the fight. On that night, Saul, seeing that something was wrong, had lots drawn, and Jonathan was taken. Then came the first clash between the prince and his father, Jonathan saying ironically, "I did but taste a little honey .....and lo, I must die." The wilful king replied, "Thou shalt surely die, Jonathan."

Saul immediately discovered that there was such a thing as public sentiment, and that it was stronger than the royal power. Many kings after his day were to ascertain the same fact—what a pity that there were not more instances! We do not know who the spokesman was on this occasion; perhaps angry resentment found many voices. The people said that not one hair of

Jonathan's head should fall to the ground—and the king found it advisable not to press the matter. This is one of the first cases in history when public sentiment manifested itself successfully against the ruling authority, and, as such, deserves this especial mention.

Saul was an able military leader, and the Israelites were frequently victorious under his leadership. When he defeated the Amalekites, he did not fulfill to the letter the stern directions of the voice of the Lord, who through Samuel told him to kill the women, the babies, the sucklings in their mothers' arms, and all the valuable cattle. (Wicked Amalekite babies!)

Unfortunately, Saul was not moved by any pity, for the children were slaughtered; King Agag was spared out of royal courtesy, and the best of the cattle were saved, ostensibly to offer up to Jehovah, but probably for more practical purposes. Saul was always afraid of Samuel; he had the attitude of a bad boy toward a severe private tutor; but the reason he gave Samuel for sparing the cattle is significant, coming so soon after the public demonstration about Jonathan: "I feared the people, and obeyed their voice." Saul could not bear to see Samuel leaving him, and with his powerful hand he clutched the robe of the prophet, which tore in his grasp, Samuel using the rent as an allegory of the rending of Saul's kingdom.

Samuel relented at Saul's despairing plea, but it was an unfortunate decision for Agag. It is a vivid scene, when the king of the Amalekites, who now believed in his reprieve, came toward Samuel, walking delicately, with self-conscious, embarrassed and mincing steps, saying, "Surely the bitterness of death is past." They were his last words, for Samuel immediately dissected him.

Samuel was an incorruptible Judge; and the fact that he took pride in what we regard to-day as a matter of course would seem to indicate that high officials in Israel were not always what they should be, probably on the whole decidedly inferior to court officials in the twentieth century. Samuel said to the people, "I am old and gray-headed.....and I have walked before you from my childhood unto this day."

Behold, here I am:.....whom have I defrauded? whom have I oppressed? or of whose hand have I received any bribe to blind mine eyes therewith? and I will restore it you.

After a number of chapters dealing with the adventures of Saul and of David, one forgets Samuel, and it is with a shock that the twenty-fifth chapter opens with the words, "And Samuel died." One feels that a pillar of the house is fallen, and that calamity will visit Israel in his absence.

Samuel is the only authentic ghost in the Bible; the only spirit who rose from the grave in palpable form, spoke definite words, and returned to his slumber. King Saul's visit to the medium has a strangely modern air. It was the last night of his life; he had well-founded fears that on the morrow he would be defeated by the Philistines. He missed sadly the counsel of his old tutor; and he enquired of God by dreams, by casting lots, and by prophets; all in vain. As a last resort, he visited a medium, the witch of Endor; once more his story reminds us of Macbeth.

The mediums were strictly forbidden by law; it was a capital offence to practice the art. But the desire of human nature to communicate with spirits was then and is now so strong that no legal measures or no power of reasoning can stop the traffic. Saul went in the darkness of the night, and in disguise, and when the woman asked him with whom he would like to speak, he said in a voice of authority (which betrayed his identity), "Bring me up Samuel." To the amazement of the old witch, who had hitherto relied on hocus-pocus, Samuel actually appeared. She cried out, "An old man cometh up; and he is covered with a mantle." Death had not changed the character of the old prophet; he that was holy was holy still. He asked sternly why Saul had broken into his quiet sleep; Saul replied pathetically (and our hearts go out to him) : "I am sore distressed; for the Philistines make war against me, and God is departed from me." Samuel informed him that everything had happened as he had predicted (I told you so), and then added grimly, "Tomorrow shalt thou and thy sons be with me."

Saul fainted. The next day the battle went sore against him. The loyal Jonathan fell, fighting for his father's kingdom. Saul himself was cruelly wounded by the Philistine archers, and asked his armour-bearer to put an end to his sufferings; the boy was afraid, so Saul, like an old Roman, fell on his own sword.

The character of the First King is not impeccable, but he was very human, and had the faults that mark the natural man. The happiest years of his life came in his careless youth, riding over the hills after the herds; there was nothing kingly about him except his appearance. His jealousy of David is quite natural; the girls sang, Saul has killed his thousands, and David his ten thousands. He could hardly be expected to hear that song with enthusiasm. I suppose there are some ministers of the gospel who, if they should hear a song proclaiming that they had saved a thousand souls, while their successors in the pastorate had saved ten thousand, might, in their glad rejoicing over the addition to the elect, feel some tincture of pique. Saul's jealousy of young David was further inflamed by the fact that his own children were mad about his rival; Jonathan loved him to distraction, and Saul's daughter Michal fell in love with him. Saul was no more vain and no more jealous than the average American.

He had no genius for government; he was more captain than statesman. He was rash and impulsive, given to outbursts of passion, followed by hearty repentance. He was subject to terrible fits of depression, nervous melancholia so severe and so prolonged that he lay as if in a stupour. The only thing that could help him then was music, of which he was inordinately fond. We have seen how, when he heard the orchestra playing with the prophets, he went into an ecstasy; so when this cloud of despondency darkened his mind, David came and played music—perhaps the old cowboy tunes—and he was refreshed and took up his work again. No one has ever understood this peculiar melancholy either then or now; the Bible diagnoses it as possession by an evil spirit, which well describes its effects; this evil spirit could be banished only by music, the method so familiar to-day in the treatment of nervous diseases. Browning has poetically recreated the effect on Saul of David's music.

Looking back on Saul's life and career, it does not appear that he was either sensual or vindictive, the two most common vices of monarchs; indeed, he was rather like a big, grown-up boy, incapable of dealing with problems of state. In comparison with the average character of kings, both in ancient and in modern history, Saul meets the test rather well.

VI

KING DAVID

Neither Saint nor Superman—Multiform Ability—His Radiant Youth—The Combat With Goliath—The Sonata — David Embarrassed by Popularity—His Friendship With Prince Jonathan—His Marriage With Princess Michal—Their Quarrel and Separation—Saul's Anger at the Dinner Table—Parting of David and Jonathan—The Lie to Ahimelech and Its Consequences—David's Simulation of Madness—A Leader of Sedition—The Pretty New Wife—Lamentation of David for Saul and Jonathan—Ishboshetk the King—His Assassination—David Monarch of All He Surveyed—His Kindness to Mephibosheth and Its Sequel—David's Sin and Crime—Nathan the Bold—The Rebellion of Prince Absalom—Character of General Joab—David's Grief for His Son—Murder of Amasa—David's Feeble Old Age—Presumption of Prince Adonijah—Summary of David's Character— Personality of David.

David was neither a saint nor a superman; he was an epitome of manhood. He was a representative of masculinity, and had the virtues and vices that often accompany virility. Physically, mentally, spiritually he may stand as the genius of his race. Leave David out of the Bible, there would be vast empty spaces. In his own person he represents the athlete, the shepherd, the poet, the musician, the mystic, the man-of-war, the father, the friend, and the statesman. His deeds, his poems, and his prayers are alike immortal. In spite of his gross sins, he had a certain greatness of heart that drew the love of men and women who knew him, that still commands the affection and homage of those who read the story of his life. As a shepherd lad, he was the incarnation of the strength, beauty, and grace of youth. King Saul commanded his servants to bring to the court a first-class musician.

Then answered one of the servants, and said, Behold, I have seen a son of Jesse the Bethlehemite, that is cunning in playing, and a mighty valiant man, and a man of war, and prudent in matters, and a comely person, and the Lord is with him.

When Saul's incompetence became manifest, Samuel was forced by the divine voice to commit high treason, to appoint a new king while the throne was still occupied. It would seem that there was then a higher duty than obedience to the reigning power. Samuel called Jesse to a sacrifice, and passed his numerous sons in review. The first one, Eliab, was a superb creature, of such imposing face and figure that Samuel said to himself, This is the man. But the Voice whispered to him that the true value is not in outward appearance, but in the heart. It was a handsome family, the family of Jesse; and the proud father ordered his seven sons to stand in succession before the prophet. It is like a fairy story, where the obscure and neglected child turns out to be the favourite of fortune. Samuel was puzzled; he asked Jesse if these were all the sons he had. It appeared that Jesse had not thought it worth while to bring the youngest, who was out keeping the sheep.

And he sent, and brought him in. Now he was ruddy, and withal of a beautiful countenance, and goodly to look to.

To the amazement of the brothers, who, however, seem to have behaved better than the brothers of Joseph, young David was anointed king in the presence of the family.

David had not wasted those long days in the pasture; he had become an accomplished musician, he had composed much poetry, and he had discovered his prodigious strength in killing a predatory lion and a bear with his hands. Best of all, he had had many hours of quiet reflection and thought; in the solitude of nature, in communion with the hills, he had drawn close to God.

At the first interview, Saul did not dream that the boy was to be his successor; he saw only a radiant youth, who had come to charm his sad mind with music. He loved him at first sight, kept him in his presence, and made him his armour-bearer.

David's first exploit was to destroy the Philistine heavyweight champion, Goliath. He was an enormous fellow. His height was six cubits and a span. Now we do not know exactly how long the Bible cubit is, but it is safe to call it about twenty inches; and the span was probably half a cubit, so that the gentleman from Gath was ten feet six—a tall man in any company. He was as strong as he was tall; for his breastplate weighed one hundred and fifty pounds, and the tip of his spear weighed twenty pounds. Standing straight in shining armour, it is safe to say that he would have attracted attention anywhere.

He came out in front of his countrymen every day for forty days, and every time he challenged the children of Israel to produce a champion to contend with him, that they might have a fight to a finish. Every morning and every evening he made his little speech, until the Israelites found the repetition extremely tiresome; but as no one seemed eager to accept Goliath's invitation, the situation continued without noticeable alteration.

David's three big brothers were in Saul's army; the boy had gone back to feed his father's sheep. Jesse sent him to the camp with food from the farm for his brothers, a fine present for their captain, and bade him return with news of the family. As David drew near to the trench, he saw the host moving out in battle array, and their singing and shouting fired his young blood. Then, to his surprise, the big Philistine stepped out, made his customary remarks, and the Israelites fled from his presence. David shot questions right and left, and soon learned all there was to know; also of the glorious reward that would be given to anyone who could eliminate the giant. His oldest brother Eliab heard him talking, and was disgusted. This is no place for a boy; what do you mean by leaving your sheep? I know what's the matter with you; you have sneaked off from home and your work, to see the battle; now get back as fast as you can. But this big-brother sneer made little impression on David, for he was full of a great plan. He talked so volubly that Saul sent for him; and the king must have laughed outright when David told him that he would fight the Philistine. But his boyish eloquence so moved the monarch that he won permission.

Goliath looked more like a fighting-machine than like a human being; but as we know to-day that a fifty-thousand-ton battleship can be destroyed by one torpedo, so David knew that if he could hit Goliath in an unprotected place with his sling-shot, it would be all over with the big champion. He had had plenty of time to practice, and had become as skilful as many an American boy to-day; and he went forth with his small but dangerously offensive weapon. As for his defensive armour, that was in his feet; he took off Saul's cumbrous suit of mail, for if he did not succeed in hitting the Philistine, he did not want anything to interfere with his speed in running away. He knew that Goliath was not dressed for sprinting.

The disgust of the giant when he saw the fairfaced boy advancing found expression in words; but David was also a good talker, and after a slanging match, he took careful aim, and hit the big face with the first shot, so that Goliath was knocked out. Before he could recover consciousness, David was upon him, and killed him with his own sword. It must be granted that in this exploit David exhibited more skill than courage; but when you are in opposition to superior strength, you must use your wits, like Jack-the-Giant-killer.

It is pleasant to remember that the composer Johann Kuhnau (1660-1722), who immediately preceded Bach as organist of St. Thomas's church in Leipzig, and was the originator of the sonata as a composition in movements, wrote six sonatas called *Musical Representation of Some Bible Stories*. The piece dealing with David and Goliath is more quaint than impressive, but it gives delight still. As it is not generally known, the separate movements—real programme music—are worth transcribing.

1. The stamping and defying of Goliath.
2. The terror of the Israelites and their prayer to God at the sight of their terrible enemy.
3. The courage of David, his desire to humble the pride of the giant, and his child-like faith in God.
4. The contest of words between David and Goliath, and the combat, in which Goliath, wounded in the forehead by a stone from the sling of David, falls to the ground and is slain.
5. The flight of the Philistines, pursued and slain with the sword by the Israelites.
6. The exultation of the Israelites over their victory.
7. The praise of David, sung by the women in alternate choirs.
8. The general joy and triumph expressing itself in hearty dancing and leaping.

Just as the Bible has been the quarry for hundreds of stage-plays, so it affords excellent material for instrumental music.

The dismay of the Philistines was equalled only by the joy of the Israelites; and from that moment until his death, David was a popular hero. Saul gave him a high command in the army, and might have continued to love him if the women had not gone out to meet David with singing and dancing and an odious comparison. "And Saul eyed David from that day forward." On the morrow Saul had one of his attacks of melancholia, and as David was playing music in his presence, Saul hurled a javelin at him; but he was not so good a shot as the young man, for he missed him twice.

Like many another, David found his popularity embarrassing, for he knew that the king would never forgive him; he behaved with modesty and tact, and the splendid loyalty that he had perhaps inherited from his great-grandmother made him true to Saul to the end; but it was all in vain. For the more modestly he behaved, the more the people loved him and the more violent and uncontrollable became the jealousy of the king.

David lived at court; and there began that noble and beautiful friendship between Jonathan and David that has added to the beauty of the Bible and to the glory of human nature. Few things can exceed in duration true friendship between man and man; as it has no physical foundation, it does not easily decay. It is interesting to remember that David's friendship with the king's son lasted forever; whereas his love for the king's daughter, whom he took in marriage, burned out and became extinct. Princess Michal loved David, her maids told Saul about it, and he was pleased; for he saw a way of destroying him. He told his servants to let David know that he was to become the king's son-in-law; David of course made a modest disclaimer, saying that he could provide no worthy marriage settlement. Then, inspired by Saul, they told him that if he would kill a hundred Philistines, the deed would be accepted as dowry. The intention was of course to have the rash young man lose his life in the attempt. But David went out with his own company and slew two hundred; so Michal became his wife. His popularity increased enormously; in the quaint Bible phrase, "his name was much set by."

Throwing the javelin seems to have been Saul's favorite indoor sport, though he was an indifferent shot; he once more missed David, the weapon quivering in the wall, and he missed his son Jonathan at close range. Perhaps he was too angry to shoot straight. Then he planned to kill David in his bed; but Michal let her husband down through a window, and put a dummy in his place, pretending to her father that David had threatened her if she would not connive at his escape. It is interesting to observe that this dummy was the ikon, or family god, showing that the Israelites were forever breaking the second commandment.

It is a pity that this marriage, which began as a love-match, should have ended in a quarrel, but the cause of the separation was quite natural. Michal must have been an attractive woman, for after Saul quarrelled with David, the king gave her to a new husband by the name of Phalti, who was so uxorious that when later he was forced to deliver her back to David, he followed behind her—poor fellow—weeping. He made such a noise that Captain Abner peremptorily ordered him to go home, like a dog whose services are no longer required.

And her husband went with her along weeping behind her to Bahurim. Then said Abner unto him, Go, return. And he returned.

Some time after this, King David was coming from a victory, bringing back the ark of God. He was in such high spirits that he danced before the Lord with all his might, very scantily dressed; as the procession entered the city, Michal looked out of a window, and there, to her disgust, she saw her husband the king leaping and dancing in the street. With that regard for conventional decency so much stronger in women than in men, she despised him; she thought he was making a fool of himself. It is easy to understand her rage and shame; no woman likes to have her husband make himself ridiculous. When David came into the house in bright glee and wholly satisfied with himself, his wife greeted him in a manner that first amazed and then infuriated him. She told him acidly that he had made a vulgar and silly exhibition, that everyone was secretly laughing at him. "You thought you were just wonderful, didn't you? Well, you made an ass out of yourself." David's male pride was horribly hurt; he answered brutally, and as so often happens in domestic quarrels, he insulted her family, reminding her cruelly that he had been chosen over her father; that he was better than any person in her father's house. Now he was going to do as he pleased; he would dance even more vilely than she had seen him. This was the end; he never spoke to her again. Unfortunate, but human.

Such is the power of the tongue. David had not hesitated to take her back from an intervening husband; his pride, which had not recoiled from that, could not forgive her ridicule.

When David saw that everything he did only increased Saul's anger, he had a long talk with Jonathan about it, and the two young men swore eternal friendship, Jonathan begging David not to forget his children when they were fatherless. He seems to have been certain of the speedy approach of disaster to the king, and he knew that he must fall with his father, like a loyal prince of the house. It is pleasant to observe that he never joined David in public opposition to the king, though doubtless he wished to do so. At this time they arranged a system of signals. To-morrow was the feast of the new moon; and David knew that his absence from table would be observed, though he did not dare to be present. The dinner-time came; Saul took his accustomed seat by the wall, and Abner, the captain of the host, sat at his side; the king glared at David's empty place, but said nothing. On the second day, however, he asked Jonathan what had become of David, for he knew well enough that Jonathan could tell him, if he would. The prince began to defend his friend, and Saul threw a javelin across the table at him; Jonathan rose, wild with rage, and walked out, leaving his dinner untasted. The next day, by a previously arranged signal, Jonathan went out in the field with a lad carrying his arrows, ostensibly to practise marksmanship; but David was hidden. When Jonathan shot the arrows beyond the place where his friend lay, and told the boy to pick them up, David knew that the king was obdurate. The boy took the bow and arrows and returned to the city. No sooner had he disappeared than David sprang up; the two friends embraced, and renewed their vows of friendship in one of the most deeply affecting scenes to be found in literature. Jonathan returned to the city and David wandered off into exile; it is impossible to say which of them suffered most.

David went away to Nob, and there asked Ahimelech the high priest for food and weapons, telling him a lie, saying that he was an emissary of Saul, and that the king's business required haste. Ahimelech loved David, and gave him the communion-bread and the huge sword of the dead Goliath, which David was apparently able to swing. All might have been well if a certain man named Doeg, devoted to Saul, had not happened to be there. He informed against David; the king sent for Ahime-lech, who came with the priests; despite his protestations of innocence, Saul ordered the footmen to slay the whole company; they did not dare to commit this sacrilege, but Doeg had no scruples, and single-handed he butchered eighty-five of the holy and defenceless men. Many centuries later, the poet Dryden helped to hand Doeg down to infamy.

One of Ahimelech's sons escaped, and told David the tragic news; David was overwhelmed with remorse because of his lie. He said, "I knew Doeg would tell, when I saw him there. I am now guilty of the death of all the members of your family." But the young man knew he was safer with David than anywhere else, so he accompanied him on his wanderings—one more evidence of the confidence that David inspired in those who knew him.

Although David behaved toward Saul with forbearance and loyalty, the king was determined to make it a case of civil war. He proclaimed David to be a public enemy, and pursued him with the royal army. Curiously enough, David fled to Achish, the king of Gath, the old home of Goliath; he was immediately recognised by the people, and he simulated madness; he "scrabbled on the doors of the gate, and let his spittle fall down upon his beard." He was a good actor, and completely deceived King Achish, who exclaimed in a fashion that is not without humour. David was brought before his presence as a dangerous enemy, but his crazy behaviour was so convincing that the king said:

Lo, ye see the man is mad: wherefore then have ye brought him to me? Have I need of mad men, that ye have brought this fellow to play the mad man in my presence? shall this fellow come into my house?

Although David was in reality no rebel, he was generally so regarded; his father and his brothers joined him, which must have taken considerable courage; and a natural thing happened.

And everyone that was in distress, and everyone that was in debt, and everyone that was discontented, gathered themselves unto him; and he became a captain over them: and there were with him about four hundred men.

He must have been disgusted with this rag, tag, and bobtail of an army, but there was no help for it; his life was in daily danger. He was the fox, and the royal pack of hounds chased him from cover to cover.

Several times he could have killed Saul; but he loved the king, and had a sacred reverence for the office. Once he cut off a piece of Saul's cloak, and at a safe distance held it up to the sight of the king, as proof of his loyalty. He also made a flattering speech, trying to prove to Saul that he was making much ado about nothing.

After whom is the king of Israel come out? after whom dost thou pursue? after a dead dog, after a flea?

This time Saul wept, and repented, saying, Is this thy voice, my son David? And for a time they were reconciled.

While still in exile, David, in a dramatic manner, obtained a new and beautiful wife. It seems that he and his followers had protected the vast property of a rich farmer named Nabal; being in need of food, David sent his young men to this plutocrat, requesting assistance. Nabal was a hard-bitten old skinflint, and he said, Who is David? Am I going to hand over my goods to a runaway servant? When this message was brought back, the impulsive and passionate young leader flew into a tempest of rage and sallied out to destroy Nabal, his family and his entire possessions. There is no doubt that he would have done this if it had not been for Nabal's pretty wife Abigail. She secretly took an enormous heap of costly provisions, and went to meet the avenger. David was extremely susceptible to beauty, and when this "woman of good understanding and of a beautiful countenance" looked him in the eyes and spoke flatteringly and soothingly, he melted like snow in the sunshine. She was as fair in speech as in face; she said: "The soul of my lord shall be bound in the bundle of life with the Lord thy God." David blessed her for coming, and for saving him from the guilt of murder. She returned home.

That night old Nabal gave a big dinner to his cronies, and got very drunk. He was feeling bad the next morning, but so much worse when his wife told him of her doings that he had a stroke, and in ten days was dead. David exclaimed with delight when he heard of this, and immediately asked Abigail to become his wife. She accepted with alacrity.

There were two fine qualities in David that were never understood even by those closest to him; one was his reverential loyalty to King Saul, the other the strength of his family affection. Both were greater than his concern for his personal glory or safety. Nearly all men have been glad to learn of the death of their enemies, especially when an immediate advantage rises from it. Julius Caesar and David—both humane—are the notable exceptions. David was at Ziklag one day when a messenger came from the field of battle, bearing the news that Saul was dead and saying that he, the messenger, had, at the king's request, killed him. To the astonishment of the visitor, David was struck with horror. Wast thou not afraid to stretch forth thine hand to destroy the Lord's anointed? And he had the man killed on the spot.

Then he composed an elegiac poem for Saul and Jonathan, which, in immortal phrase, sets forth the passion of loyalty and friendship:

The beauty of Israel is slain upon thy high places: how are the mighty fallen! Tell it not in Gath, publish it not in the streets of Askelon; lest the daughters of the Philistines rejoice, lest the daughters of the uncircumcised triumph......
Saul and Jonathan were lovely and pleasant in their lives, and in their death they were not divided: they were swifter than eagles, they were stronger than lions......
How are the mighty fallen in the midst of the battle! O Jonathan, thou wast slain in thine high places.

I am distressed for thee, my brother Jonathan; very pleasant hast thou been unto me: thy love to me was wonderful, passing the love of women. How are the mighty fallen, and the weapons of war perished!

Saul's son, Ishbosheth, was crowned king of Israel, and David king of Judah. Civil war began, and nearly all the forty years of David's reign were filled with fighting against foreign and domestic foes. Two famous generals were Abner, who was a true and high-minded gentleman, and Joab, a professional fighting-hack, who understood neither pity nor remorse, and who never forgot a personal enemy. Abner was of the party of Israel, for he had been Saul's captain-in-chief; in the early days of the civil war, the three sons of Zeruiah— Joab, Abishai, and young Asahel—pursued hard after the retreating Abner. Now Asahel was the fastest runner in the country; he gained rapidly on Abner, who besought him to stop, or at any rate to take armour from one of the young men, so that there might be a fair duel. But he kept on in hot pursuit; and Abner, much against his will, was forced in self-defence to slay him, pushing his long spear backward.

After this battle, Abner pleaded with Joab to end the strife; and Joab pretended that all was well. Meanwhile the loyal Abner was insulted by the idiotic Ishbosheth, so grossly insulted that he went over to David. Then Joab treacherously invited Abner to a quiet conference, and slew him at the gate. King David wept bitterly, gave Abner a royal funeral, and mourned publicly at the grave, saying that a prince and a great man had fallen in Israel, adding, "These sons of Zeruiah be too hard for me."

King Ishbosheth was assassinated, killed in his bed, and the murderers brought his head to the horrified David, who reminded them of what he had done to the messenger who came from dead Saul, "who thought that I would have given him a reward for his tidings."

How much more, when wicked persons have slain a righteous person in his own house upon his bed?

He gave orders; the messengers were killed, their bodies mutilated, and hanged over the pool in Hebron.

David was then anointed king over Israel; he reigned seven years over Judah and thirty-three years over the united countries. Jerusalem became the seat of the monarchy and the city of David.

His power grew apace; he formed an alliance with Hiram king of Tyre, and his conquests extended so far that he was able to put a garrison in Damascus, the Syrians paying tribute. Garrisons were also placed in Edom, and the army became a highly efficient force, under the command of General Joab.

It is pleasant to remember King David's kindness to a son of Jonathan, who was a cripple. This was Mephibosheth, who was permanently injured, as so many babies have been, by the carelessness of a nurse. He was five years old, when the news of the death of his father and grandfather came; his nurse picked him up, started to run and, in her haste, dropped him. As a result, he was incurably lame in both feet. Years later, David enquired if there was anyone left of the house of Saul, to whom he might show a kindness for Jonathan's sake; a man named Ziba appeared and told the king of Mephibosheth. The lame young man appeared in the royal presence with fear and trembling, and did obeisance; but David told him that he would always care for him for his father's sake; he should receive back the property that he would have inherited from Saul, and he should be a perpetual guest at the king's own table. Mephibosheth was overcome with embarrassed gratitude, and said: "What is thy servant, that thou shouldest look upon such a dead dog as I am?" But David commanded Ziba and his whole family to work for Mephibosheth with the same zeal and reverence as if he were King Saul himself; and as Ziba had fifteen sons and twenty servants, it was a large order. Ziba cheerfully obeyed the king's directions; Mephibosheth and his baby son Micha were treated with the homage due to royalty. David never appeared to better advantage; he not only saved Mephibosheth and his family from want, but he restored the poor cripple's self-respect. From being a neglected and helpless fugitive, he held a high place in the palace of the king, and it is certain that no one dared to slight him.

It turned out later that either Mephibosheth or Ziba was a liar; it is one of those innumerable cases that depend on human testimony, the least dependable thing in the whole world; the testimony is flatly contradictory and both puzzled and disgusted David, so that he finally settled the matter with a contemptuous gesture. It seems incredible, after David's kindness, that Mephibosheth should have behaved with rank and treacherous ingratitude; but it would not be the first or the last time in history. When David was in sore distress during the rebellion of Absalom, and the opportunists were in doubt which side to support, Ziba appeared before the king with an immense store of provisions, and in response to David's question as to Mephibosheth, Ziba replied that the lame man stayed in Jerusalem, rejoicing in David's downfall, and believing that the house of Saul would regain the throne. This sounds like a huge lie; but David apparently believed it, for he told Ziba that the property of Mephibosheth should thenceforth belong to him. After Absalom's death, when King David re-entered Jerusalem, who should come to meet him but Mephibosheth, looking like a vagabond; he had neither dressed his feet, nor trimmed his beard, nor washed his clothes from the day David had fled. This looked like sincerity of mourning; and the king enquired, Why did you not go with me, Mephibosheth? and he answered that he had planned to ride to the king, but that Ziba had slandered him. In this mental morass, the king floundered a moment, and then said impatiently that the property must be divided between Ziba and Mephibosheth. The latter answered humbly that he was willing to have Ziba take all, he was so happy at the king's successful return. All we can say is, Somebody lied.

If Mephibosheth continued to eat at the king's table, the situation must have been somewhat constrained.

It is sad that after recording the fidelity of David to the memory of his best friend, we should have also to write down one of the blackest crimes of his life. But although David is one of the heroes of Israelitish history, the honest old chronicler set down the most damaging facts, for only one reason —because they were the truth. David's adultery and murder have made a tremendous impression on the world, just as Napoleon's murder of the Duc D'Enghien has shocked people more than the hundred thousand murders he committed to satisfy his selfish ambition; what should one individual be among so many? But most readers have so little imagination that the fate of one well-known person of high social position stirs them more than thousands of nameless sufferers; just as we are more distressed at an automobile accident that happens before our eyes than we are by reading of a faraway calamity that destroys two hundred or two thousand people. David had much wholesale slaughter on his soul besides this particular crime; but here we know the names of the characters, and they are as real as acquaintances.

Toward the close of a summer day, after David had been enjoying a siesta, he rose and walked on the roof of the royal palace; and in the dusk, he saw a woman bathing. He sent a messenger to inquire her name, and upon learning that she was married to Uriah the Hittite, he took her himself. It has often been the royal prerogative to take anything that happens at the moment to seem attractive; one reason why so many kings have no true appreciation of beauty is because admiration with them is always mingled with predatory desire; they have about as much artistic discernment of beauty as a thief has of the beauty of the plate and jewels he steals. He sent Bathsheba home again, and after a time she sent him word that she was with child. Her husband Uriah was away with the army, fighting for his country, which does not add to the attractiveness of David's conduct. The king sent word to General Joab that he wished to speak with Uriah. Accordingly, the soldier, who seems to have been a rugged, upstanding man-at-arms, came into the presence of the king. In vain did David attempt to persuade Uriah to go to his house; Uriah said that his comrades were fighting at the field, and he would be ashamed to sleep in comfort while they were in hardship and peril. Doubtless this was not the real reason; he must have suspected the truth the moment he looked into the king's face. So David sent the brave fellow back to the camp, with instructions to Joab to put him in the most dangerous position in the battle. Joab knew what was expected and why; and in the dispatch he sent home it appeared that among the casualties was Uriah the Hittite. The greedy monarch then married Bathsheba; but although he forgot God, God did not forget him.

Nathan, the prophet of Jehovah, appeared before David and told him a pathetic story of the cupidity and cruelty of a rich man in dealing with a poor and defenceless person; the king's anger was aroused —we always despise our own wickedness when we see it in others or on the stage—and said that the rich man must die. Then Nathan pointed his finger at the king and said, *Thou art the man.* He prophesied three evils that would come upon David, because of his sin: the sword should never depart from his house, his own wives should be publicly dishonoured by another man, and his child by Bathsheba should die. All three came true.

The only creditable part of this melancholy story is David's behaviour to Nathan. Instead of striking him down, or rebuking him, or trying to explain his own conduct, he said frankly, "I have sinned." He confessed and he repented. In spite of the care of the royal specialists, the child died, and David said, "I shall go to him, but he shall not return to me."

He kept his wife Bathsheba, for what would have been her position if he had sent her away? She always retained her influence over him, and later became the mother of King Solomon.

Little pleasure had David in his children: little pleasure in anything. As in the life of Saul, the careless days of his youth were the only happy ones he knew. In order to retain his throne, and to save Israel from foreign domination, he could never sheathe the sword; bloodshed was chronic.

Prince Absalom inherited the manly beauty of the house of Jesse: "from the sole of his foot even to the crown of his head there was no blemish in him." Especially noticeable was his magnificent hair; it was so thick and glossy that every year when he had it cut it was like taking a harvest off a field. But he had no more moral sense than Alcibiades; he was a traitor to his father and to the nation. He stole away the hearts of the people by promises as fair as his face; and finally he felt himself strong enough to organise open rebellion. The uprising was so general that David left the holy city in shame and disgrace, like a hunted man with a price on his head. But in a decisive battle, in which the king's forces were led by the two sons of Zeruiah—Joab and Abishai—Absalom's forces were routed. Before the battle, David gave public orders that no harm must come to the person of Absalom; as so often happens in tragic quarrels between fathers and sons, the father loves his child with a passionate intensity greater than in harmonious days. Anyone who has observed life must have seen this, which, if we did not know something of the strange workings of the human heart, would be indeed a mystery.

Joab was a plain fighting man; he saw in Absalom the most dangerous foe of the state, and when the retreating prince was caught by the head in the boughs of a great oak, Joab slew him with no more compunction than one would kill a rattlesnake.

The king sat between the two gates, awaiting news from the front; he was far more interested in the welfare of Absalom than in his own kingdom. The watchman, standing aloft, saw a man running alone, followed soon by another, Ahimaaz arrived first, and shouted joyously the news of the great victory; but the king enquired, Is the young man Absalom safe? Ahimaaz did not dare tell him, but muttered something about a great tumult, the significance of which he had not waited to know. Then Cushi arrived in the same spirit of exultation; and the king asked, Is the young man Absalom safe? Cushi, with diplomatic tact, replied, May the enemies of the king all be as that young man now is. The overwhelming grief in David's heart left no room for any other emotion; his personal gain was forgotten in the loss of his selfish and cruel son. No cry of anguish that has come down from all the immeasurable woe of the past is more poignant than David's lamentation:

O my son Absalom, my son Absalom! would God I had died for thee, O Absalom, my son, my son!

The years of imperial pride and glory, which have made monsters out of so many men, had never hardened the nature of David; the tenderness of his heart was ever greater than his ambition.

General Joab was disgusted with David's behaviour, and told him exactly what he thought of it. David had never liked Joab or his family, and he did not forget this speech, which was like a knife in a green wound. He appointed Amasa in Joab's place; but he did not live to take it. Joab came up to Amasa affectionately, and said, "Art thou in health, my brother?" took him by the beard to kiss him, and with the other hand ran him through. Amasa wallowed in blood in the midst of the highway; a crowd gathered about his dead body, for this cold-hearted and treacherous murder shocked the whole nation.

Joab retained his position as Captain of the host, and David seems to have been afraid of him; but after a long career of fighting loyally for the king, his good sense deserted the old soldier at last, and he made the fatal mistake of supporting Prince Adonijah, who, in David's old age, rebelled against his father, and announced himself king. David was too feeble to exert himself; but Bathsheba came in, and reminded him of his promise that Solomon should be his heir. He therefore made a public proclamation to that effect, which caused such general rejoicing that the followers of Adonijah disappeared like a mist, and left him in ridiculous isolation.

On his deathbed, David sent for Solomon and said, as Joshua had said before him:

I go the way of all the earth: be thou strong therefore, and shew thyself a man: And keep the charge of the Lord thy God, to walk in His ways.....as it is written in the law of Moses.

He left two death warrants for Solomon to execute; one for Joab, and one for Shimei, a blackguard who had cursed him during the temporary success of Absalom. But those who then stood by him were to be remembered in kindness by his son.

No figure in history is more real than David; he stands before us, with his grandeur and his littleness, his virtues and his crimes. No warrior was ever more beloved by the mighty men who fought for him, and the episode where he refused to drink of the water that his captains had brought to him at the risk of their lives—for they had to fight their way to the well, and then fight their way back, spilling blood without spilling water—is perhaps the most charming in his career; for it shows not only the greatness, but the fineness of his nature.

No modern historian, whatever his personal bias, can injure David or blacken his memory, for the simple reason that we already know the worst that can be said against him; the Bible does not spare him. But in the opinion of most unprejudiced readers, David is not only an imposing but an attractive personality; we admire the great king and we love the true-hearted man.

VII

SOLOMON IN ALL HIS GLORY—THE ROMANTIC FIGURE OF ELIJAH

The Last Days of David—Prosperity of Israel Under Solomon—Executions of Adonijah, Joab and Shimei—Solomon's Dream—His First Court Judgment—Building of the Temple— Other Construction Work—The Visit of the Queen of Sheba— Her Amazement at the Luxury of Solomon's Court and State Dinners—Dedication of the Temple—Solomons Fall From Grace Through Women—The Radical Leader Jeroboam—Solomon's Death—Rehoboam's Method in Suppressing Discontent— The Revolution—The Division into Two Kingdoms—Bloody Days in Israel—King Ahab and His Terrible Queen—Literary Splendour of the Narrative—Appearance of the Prophet Elijah—The Long Drought—The Contest with the Prophets of Baal— The Rain—Jezebel's Threat and Elijah's Flight—His Despair and his Visions—Naboth and His Vineyard—The Espionage Act—Ahab Confronted with Elijah—His Fate Foretold—His Repentance—Johoshaphat, King of Judah—His Alliance with Ahab—The Plan for War on Syria—Gathering of the Soothsayers—The Holy Prophet Micaiah—Defeat and Death of Ahab—The Last Hours of Elijah—His Prophecy to King Ahaziah—The Two Captains and Their Disastrous Mission— Elijah and Elisha—The Last Walk Together—The Chariot of Fire—The Falling Mantle—Character of Elijah.

The last days of David are depressing to contemplate; the old lion was sick and helpless and at the mercy of women. Rebellions and fighting brought the smell of blood even into the death-chamber, and the chilly invalid shuddered with something more than the cold. In sleepless meditation, he must often have remembered the days of his brilliant youth, his triumph over Goliath, the long talks and walks with Jonathan, and the hour when he was anointed king. If he could only have looked into the future, he would have been comforted; for then he would have known that greater than all his mighty deeds of war, more splendid than all his royal splendour, were his magnificent poems. David the fighter and David the statesman have a sincere place in history; far above them is David the Poet.

Then sat Solomon upon the throne of David his father; and his kingdom was established greatly.

Israel reached its highest point under the leadership of the Wise King; he inherited his father's common sense and literary genius. But he was forced to begin his reign by killing his brother. Among David's sons, Solomon had a monopoly of wisdom; Adonijah appears to have been a preposterous fool. No sooner had he been forgiven for attempting a *coup d'état,* than he came to Bathsheba and asked that she would beg Solomon to give him Abishag the Shunammite—who had been the old king's nurse—in marriage. Solomon kept the fifth commandment; when his mother entered the royal apartment, the young king rose, bowed down to her, and had a seat brought for her at the right hand of the throne; thus letting the courtiers have an example in etiquette. She kept her word to Adonijah, and in all seriousness put the fatal petition. Perhaps she knew exactly what would happen.

Solomon did not often lose his temper; but this time he flew into a wild rage, and said fiercely, Why not give Adonijah the kingdom also? and he ordered the instant death of the presumptuous prince. The mighty man Benaiah was Executioner; and he dispatched Adonijah with his own hand. Then it was the turn of old General Joab, who for the first time in his life, was afraid, and fled to the altar for sanctuary—like many men, having recourse to the church only when in extreme peril; it did him no good, for Benaiah slew him in the holy place. Shimei, who had cursed David, was informed that he could remain in safety so long as he stayed at home; but after awhile, his servants ran away, and he pursued them. He was therefore executed by the efficient Benaiah. With these three enemies out of his path, Solomon's throne was firmly established. One night Solomon dreamed that the Lord God appeared to him, and asked him to name the thing he most desired, and Solomon said,

Thou hast made thy servant king instead of David my father: and I am but a little child: I know not how to go out or come in....
Give therefore thy servant an understanding heart to judge thy people, that I may discern between good and bad: for who is able to judge this thy so great people?

We cannot help remembering the decision of Paris, and its consequences. He passed by wisdom to get the fairest woman for his wife, who brought general woe in her train; whereas Solomon chose wisdom, and was rewarded with seven hundred wives and three hundred concubines—who also brought disaster.

In his dream Solomon heard the Voice saying that because he had asked for wisdom rather than long life, riches, revenge or pleasure, he should become not only the wisest among the sons of men, but that his kingdom should be of unparalled splendour, so long as he kept the true faith.

Shortly after waking, Solomon had occasion to try his judicial powers. Two women came before him, with one baby, of whom each claimed to be the mother. After listening carefully to what both had to say, the king ordered a sword to be brought, and gravely proposed to divide the child into two equal portions, so that each woman might have her fair share. To one this seemed agreeable; but the other cried out: "Give her the child!" And Solomon said that it was clear who was the real mother; and she departed in peace, with her baby in her arms.

Solomon made alliances with Pharaoh, king of Egypt, and with Hiram, king of Tyre, his father's friend and admirer. These were the days of peace and prosperity, two things usually associated in fact.

Judah and Israel were many, as the sand which is by the sea in multitude, eating and drinking, and making merry......
And Judah and Israel dwelt safely, every man under his vine and under his fig tree, from Dan even to Beersheba, ail the days of Solomon.

King David had planned to build a house for God; but he was forbidden to do so, because he had been a man of blood.

Thou hast shed blood abundantly, and hast made great wars: thou shalt not build an house unto my name, because thou hast shed much blood upon the earth in my sight.
Behold, a son shall be born to thee, who shall be a man of rest. . . . He shall build an house for my name.

David reluctantly but obediently relinquished his purpose; but he felt that he ought to make some necessary preparations for the structure.

Solomon my son is young and tender, and the house that is to be builded for the Lord must be exceeding magnifical, of fame and of glory throughout all countries; I will therefore now make preparation for it. So David prepared abundantly before his death.

Then he sent for the crown prince, and gave him this solemn and affectionate admonition:

And thou, Solomon, my son, know thou the God of thy father, and serve him with a perfect heart and with a willing mind; for the Lord searcheth all hearts, and understandeth all the imaginations of the thoughts: if thou seek him, he will be found of thee: but if thou forsake him, he will cast thee off forever. Take heed now; for the Lord hath chosen thee to build an house for the sanctuary: be strong, and do it.

David left Solomon the architect's plans for the building, so the young king could begin work without delay upon the temple designed for the worship of the Lord. With the assistance of King Hiram, who sent lumber floating down in rafts along the coast, and furnished skilled carpenters, the edifice was completed in seven years. It was ninety feet long, thirty feet wide, and forty-five feet high. Solomon was an enthusiast in construction work; it took thirteen years to build his palace, and in addition he built a stately Court House, panelled in cedar, and a fine palace for his Egyptian wife. Down on the shore of the Red Sea, he constructed a Royal Navy, with expert ship-builders furnished by King Hiram.

When the holy temple was complete, it was dedicated with solemn and appropriate exercises, Solomon making a prayer in the presence of the whole congregation; it was a long and earnest petition for God's mercy toward his people. It is interesting to see that the same spiritual conception of God which had been the characteristic idea of the Hebrew religion since the days of Abraham, was clearly set forth in this prayer, so that the people might not be led into any notion of idol worship:

But will God indeed dwell on the earth? Behold, the heaven of heavens cannot contain thee: how much less this house that I have builded?

The Queen of Sheba, a country far to the South, had heard of the wisdom of Solomon, and came with a list of difficult questions, to discover if the reports of his sagacity were accurate. I wish I knew what was on this examination paper; all we know is that Solomon passed it with errorless ease.

The Queen came like a queen, with a long train of courtiers and attendants, with many camels bearing spices and gold and precious stones, presumably to make an indelible impression on the learned king; but when she saw the way things were done in Jerusalem, she felt like a country girl; "there was no more spirit in her." She confessed that she had not believed what she had heard of Solomon and his regal splendour, and therefore came to see for herself; but the half had not been told. Evidently the state dinner that Solomon arranged in her honour exceeded in luxury anything she had ever seen or heard of. Women naturally love such things; she went into a rhapsody of praise. She gave to the king whole fortunes in gold and precious stones; and in return Solomon gave her everything she asked for, "beside that which Solomon gave her of his royal bounty." I particularly like that last phrase.

The contemptuous reference to silver in the following verses is perhaps meant as a climax in the description of the grandiose court.

And all king Solomon's drinking vessels were of gold, and all the vessels of the house of the forest of Lebanon were of pure gold; none were of silver: it was nothing accounted of in the days of Solomon.

For the king had at sea a navy of Tharshish with the navy of Hiram: once in three years came the navy of Tharshish, bringing gold, and silver, ivory, and apes, and peacocks. . . .
And the king made silver to be in Jerusalem as stones, and cedars made he to be as the sycomore trees that are in the vale, for abundance.

All this was too good to last. Things began to go wrong. *Cherchez la femme.* Solomon's curiosity in women led him into many marriages with the strange daughters of Paganism, and as he grew old and more easily flattered, these women turned away his heart from the God of Israel. The other Hebrew kings nearly all remind us of David by contrast; although he was not impeccable in conduct, that same splendid loyalty which made him true to Saul and to Jonathan, showed itself most notably in his fidelity to Jehovah. He never once faltered in his religion.

This cannot be said of Solomon. The wisest man in history was changed into a fool by women, just as the strongest man had been. He not only was an apostate, he worshipped the gods that of all false gods were particularly abominable.

At this moment appears the sinister figure of Jeroboam, the son of Nabat. He was a mighty man of valour, clever and ambitious, trusted by Solomon. One day while walking in the fields outside Jerusalem, he encountered the prophet Ahijah; the holy man took a new garment, tore it into twelve pieces, and gave ten to Jeroboam, signifying that Israel was to be separated, and that Jeroboam should reign over ten tribes. He also gave the young gentleman much good advice. Jeroboam took the cloths, and rejected the counsel. Solomon heard of the favour shown to his officer, and he sought to kill him. But Jeroboam fled into Egypt, and remained in exile until the death of the king.

After forty years of undisturbed rule, Solomon died, and his son Rehoboam succeeded. As soon as the news reached Jeroboam, he came to the young king with a huge company, at Shechem, and demanded certain concessions, apparently submitting a bill of rights on behalf of the people. Rehoboam invited them to return in three days, and they would receive an answer. Then he asked the old statesmen who had sat in committee with Solomon, what he had better do. They wisely suggested a conciliatory attitude, for they knew sedition was in the air; but a group of young sycophants took the opposite view. They advised him to put on the manner of imperial arrogance, and to say "My little finger shall be thicker than my father's loins; my father hath chastised you with whips, but I will chastise you with scorpions."

As a rule, young men are more severe and more intolerant than the old, that is, in dealing with others; it takes years of experience to bring tolerance and charity.

Rehoboam, like the fool he was, followed the advice of fools, and answered the people roughly. The result was a revolution which split the nation. Jeroboam became king of Israel, reigning over ten tribes; Rehoboam king of Judah, with the tiny tribe of Benjamin in addition.

The glory departed from the Hebrew people; from now on we have a succession of wars, and rebellions; the nation lost its soul in apostasy, as many nations have; false gods became the object of fashionable worship, and there began an era of wickedness and degeneration; for as is usually the case, decay in morals followed hard upon decay in religion. In human nature, the two are inseparably joined.

Was there ever a national history written with less patriotic bias? Instead of exalting the pride and splendour of the people, the historians demonstrate their folly and wickedness and shame. Perhaps the Hebrew chronicles are the only ones who have ever consistently put God and Truth above patriotism.

In spite of his remarkable ability and industry, Jeroboam's name will always be held in infamy, not because he directed the revolution against the son of Solomon, but because it was he who led the whole nation of Israel into the worship of false gods. The historians allude to him again and again as the head and front of this offending.

Two years before the death of Jeroboam, Asa became king of Judah; he was a righteous man, and was so devoted to the worship of Jehovah that he expelled his own mother from the throne, because she persisted in idolatry. Meanwhile Israel fell into confusion and violence; their kings were consistently bad. Elah had his throne in Tirzah, and spent most of his time getting drunk; while in this condition he was assassinated by Captain Zimri, who reigned seven days. The people did not like this man, and made Captain Omri king, who laid siege to the city of Tirzah. When Zimri saw there was no chance of escape, he made a funeral pyre of his own house, setting it on fire from within, and so perished. Omri had to fight for his throne with another pretender, whom he conquered in battle and slew, and so established his claim. He made Samaria the seat of the kingdom, did evil like his predecessors, and is chiefly remembered today for having been the father of Ahab.

Ahab was a scoundrel, who cynically married Jezebel, daughter of the king of Sidon, and openly followed her religion in worshipping the Phoenician god Baal. It is in the reign of this degenerate, when all Israel seemed given over to idolatry and sensuality, that a fiery evangelist appeared, Elijah the Tishbite.

General wickedness often arouses some great protestant. Virtue and holiness are never extinct, and the extreme of fashion brings its opposite. The zeal for God in the heart of Elijah was by the prevailing scepticism and immorality fanned into flame.

From now on the narrative is magnificent. We have the dramatic contrast between the evil of society and the stern voice of the prophet of the Lord. The story takes us through thrilling adventures, proceeding from climax to climax.

We know nothing whatever of the parents or ancestors of Elijah. He came from Tishbe in Gilead, and was strange and uncouth in appearance. He was a hairy man, clad in a rough mantle. No character in history is more romantic; there is about him an air of wild and solitary grandeur. There is immense dignity in his loneliness as he stands in the midst of the frivolous court, and harshly declares God's message to the selfish king. The very name Elijah means *My God is Jehovah*.

To Ahab he predicted a drought that might last for years; no rain, no dew shall fall until I give the word. Then he went into retirement by the brook Cherith near Jordan; he drank of the brook, and his food was brought to him by ravens, who were no wilder than he. But when the brook dried, he went to a certain city, and there at the gate was a woman in widow's weeds gathering sticks. He asked her for food and water; but she was at the last extremity, and said she had left only a handful of meal and a little oil in a cruse; she was gathering sticks for a fire, that she and her son might eat their final repast, and then die. She spoke in a tone of dull despair; but Elijah told her to prepare the food for him first, and there would be left sufficient for her son. Something in the aspect of the stranger signified authority; her faith in his words was so powerful that she gave him the meal she had reserved for her son, and then, to her amazement, the provisions were miraculously renewed, and they fared well every day.

After a time her son fell into a desperate sickness, and soon gave no sign of life. She spoke bitterly to Elijah, asking him if he had come to take her boy away from her. But Elijah took the lad into the loft where he slept, placed his body against him, and the child revived. It was a happy woman who saw the prophet coming down the ladder, carrying a lively youngster in his arms. And the widow knew that Elijah was a man of God.

There was a drought for three years; King Ahab sent everywhere to find Elijah, that he might have his revenge; but the search was unsuccessful. Then one day the prophet appeared in the royal presence, and Ahab asked angrily, "Art thou he that troubleth Israel?" And he answered boldly, that it was not he, but the king, that was responsible for the general suffering. As a matter of fact, Elijah was no more responsible for the drought than the thermometer is for the temperature. Every king had his prophet, as every man has his conscience; and the prophets of God were witnesses to the Moral Order in an age of corruption; just as Truth remains true in an age of falsehood.

Elijah then confidently proposed a competitive method to discover whether Baal or Jehovah was the real God. He suggested a public trial by fire, and human nature reveals itself in the cry of the people, "It is well spoken." The contemptible mob, never having any convictions of their own, and caring little for any religion so long as they had health and money, rejoiced in a debate of this nature, which, like almost all religious controversies, appeals only to the sporting instincts. I have seen oral duels on religion in Hyde Park, the crowd looking on exactly as they would at a prize-fight; being more interested in the hits of the antagonists than in the question discussed. It is from this point of view that many read debates between public men; one reason why controversies are generally profitless.

The priests of Baal prayed about their altar all day, mocked at intervals by Elijah, who cried *Louder! Perhaps he is asleep, or away on a journey.* Finally when the patience both of the priests and of the spectators was wearing thin, Elijah invited the people to inspect his altar. It is interesting to note that he had many barrels of water poured on it, ostensibly to make the miracle more impressive. Down came the fire and devoured it all; the discomfited priests were slain by Elijah, as they now had no friends. And then, immediately after the revelation by fire came the revelation by rain. "The heaven was black with clouds and wind, and there was a great rain." The long drought broke in a tempest; Ahab drove furiously in his chariot, and Elijah, in a tension of nervous strength after the excitement of the day, tightened his belt, and ran across country before the royal chariot all the way to the gates of Jezreel.

The water that the prophet ordered poured on the altar has given rise to an interesting theory, running far back in history, but unsuspected by Mark Twain, who made of it a humorous narrative. He describes, in the mouth of a profane old sea-captain, the true explanation of the miracle. "Twelve barrels of *water? Petroleum,* sir. PETROLEUM! That's what it was! . . . the country was full of it." The Talmud hints at this; and Sir Thomas Browne, in his *Religio Medici* (1642) gravely remarks,

For our endeavours are not only to combat with doubts, but always to dispute with the Devil: the villany of that Spirit takes a hint of Infidelity from our Studies, and by demonstrating a naturality in one way, makes us mistrust a miracle in another. . . . Again, having seen some experiments of *Bitumen,* and having read far more of *Naptha,* he whispered to my curiosity the fire of the Altar might be natural; and bid me mistrust a miracle in *Elias,* when he entrenched the Altar round with Water; for that inflammable substance yields not easily unto Water, but flames in the Arms of its Antagonist.

Queen Jezebel was not present at the trial by fire; if she had been, we may be sure that she would never have allowed Elijah to slay her priests. When Ahab told her of the catastrophe, she was furious, and determined to kill her antagonist. But she made the mistake of sending a threatening message to the prophet, which gave him time to escape. He went into the wilderness and sat under a juniper tree, and for once his courage failed him, his spirit was broken; perhaps it was the reaction after his day of triumph. He asked for death, and for an answer received food—the best possible answer to such a request. The meals gave him sufficient strength for a forty days' fast in the wilderness; he reached Horeb, the Holy Mountain. There he went into a cave, but the Voice followed him, and he characteristically replied, "I have been very jealous for the Lord God of hosts: for the children of Israel have forsaken thy covenant, thrown down thine altars, and slain thy prophets with the sword; and I, even I only, am left; and they seek my life, to take it away."

He was invited to come out, and stand upon the mount. A mighty wind passed, then an earthquake, then a fire; but the Lord was not revealed this time, not even in the fire.

After these ragings of the elements, there came a still, small voice—a divine whisper. Elijah wrapped up his face, and stood at attention. He was told to anoint certain kings, and also to anoint Elisha as prophet in his own place. The choosing of Elisha may have been a rebuke to Elijah for losing hope, yet it strengthened his heart with the thought that God's messengers would steadily continue the inspired work. But the most significant statement is at the last of this communication:

Yet have I left me seven thousand in Israel, all the knees which have not bowed unto Baal, and every mouth which hath not kissed him.

Elijah thought, as so many zealous ones have thought, that he was alone; that the whole world was given over to evil; that he was necessary to the divine plan; and that after his death, God would not have a friend remaining in the whole world. But he was told that there were many who had not surrendered to error and darkness; many who were keeping the lamp alight. Reformers are surprised when they meet anyone who holds their opinions; but in the blackest ages of history there have always been a sufficient number who have kept the truth and passed it on. They are the salt of the earth.

There was a certain rich man named Naboth, who owned a magnificent vineyard, and it happened to be situated very near the royal palace at Jezreel. Every time King Ahab looked at this fine property, he broke the tenth commandment, and as he had broken the others, he felt no remorse; all he felt at this time was earth-lust. The king was so eager that he spoke directly to Naboth, saying that he wanted the vineyard for a vegetable garden; he would give in exchange a better vineyard in another locality; or if Naboth preferred, he could receive payment in cold cash. This request was of course equivalent to a command.

Naboth, like some men in the twentieth century, was both rich and religious; he had kept the Mosaic law, being one of the seven thousand; and he was especially faithful to the fifth commandment. His audacity in answering the king is even more remarkable than his faith; for he said in a manner so uncompromising that it did not conceal his contempt, "God forbid that I should give you my fathers' land."

Ahab behaved like a child whose petition for candy has been denied; he went back to his palace, lay down on the bed, turned his face to the wall, and would not come to his meals. Jezebel hovered over him, purred like a tiger-cat, and told him to rise and be merry; for she would give him the vineyard of Naboth. As there are many wives who find it convenient not to ask their husbands where the money comes from, so Ahab did not ask the queen what method was in her mind. He awaited results, having a well-founded belief in the ability of his partner.

When women are bad, they are perhaps more thorough in evil than men; men are tormented by fears and scruples, but women are more interested in things than in ideas, and go after what they want. Jezebel, like Lady Macbeth, feared the temporising and self-debating nature of her lord; she therefore took the matter in her own hands, and being as clever as she was unscrupulous, soon arranged everything to her satisfaction.

It is interesting to see that she had no difficulty in corrupting the courts; she hired two scoundrels to give false witness, and say that Naboth was unpatriotic; he had been heard to blaspheme God and the King. Any utterance against the state has been in all communities the unpardonable sin. Naboth was immediately condemned under the espionage law; mob sentiment was aroused, and the unfortunate man hustled out of the city gates and stoned to death. No doubt men, women, and children gladly assisted in this holiday performance.

When news was brought to the queen of the success of her plan, she told Ahab to go down and enjoy a walk in his new vineyard, because Naboth was no longer living. The king lost no time in going thither, but his pleasure in his new property was ruined by the presence of Elijah, who stood in the vineyard waiting for him. What a spoil-sport, what a kill-joy is Conscience! Ahab shook with both fear and rage, and said to the prophet, "Hast thou found me, O mine enemy?" The grim, hairy Tishbite answered him sternly, "I have found thee." Then he prophesied that in the place where dogs licked up the blood of Naboth, dogs should also taste the blood of the king standing before him; that Jezebel should be devoured by dogs near the wall of Jezreel.

Ahab, who lacked both courage and convictions, was smitten with terror; he rent his garments; he wore sackcloth; he fasted; and walked softly. Thus he obtained—one hardly sees why—a reprieve from immediate annihilation at the hand of Jehovah. But he was under sentence of death, and knew he was a doomed man. And every time he was caressed by Queen Jezebel, he must have seen in imagination the horrible dogs eating her body.

Jehoshaphat, the son of Asa, was king of Judah. He was a good man, and seems to have been particularly amiable. For three years there had been no war between Syria and Israel; then Jehoshaphat paid a visit in state to Ahab, and the two kings held a conference. Ahab fatuously desired to make war on Syria. In response to an enquiry, Jehoshaphat said, "I am as thou art, my people as thy people, my horses as thy horses." But he added that before putting their allied forces in battle array, it would be well to consult the prophets of the Lord. Ahab issued an order; four hundred of his own special seers assembled, and with one voice prophesied victory. But the King of Judah was not satisfied either of the wisdom or of the authority of these phrasemongers; and he enquired with a rare touch of irony, "Is there not here a prophet of the Lord besides, that we might find out the truth from him?"

Then Ahab reluctantly admitted that there was one man, Micaiah by name; he was really a prophet of the Lord. "But I hate him: for he doth not prophesy good concerning me, but evil." This naive remark expresses the true feelings of the king, and of thousands of other persons who pretend that they want advice. But Jehoshaphat made a deprecatory gesture, and said he would feel better about it if Micaiah would come.

There followed a dramatic scene. A space was cleared before the gates of Samaria; two thrones were erected, on which sat the two kings, each clad in the royal robes. A group of prophets appeared before them, and spoke of flattering style. A certain Zedekiah, histrionically gifted, had made horns of iron, and shouted, "With these shalt thou push the Syrians, until thou have consumed them." His colleagues greeted this with unanimous support and approval. Meanwhile the courtier that had been sent to fetch Micaiah, fearing that there might be an unpleasant scene, and wishing to avoid embarrassment, undertook to advise him, urging that he join in with the others, and speak fair words. But Micaiah gave the messenger to understand that he took orders only from the Lord God of Israel.

When he appeared before the two thrones, there was an ominous silence, and Ahab, in a tone that may be easily imagined, said, "Micaiah, shall we go against Ramoth-Gilead to battle, or shall we forbear?" The irony of the prophet's reply is magnificent. Seeing what was expected of him, he said tauntingly, "Go, and prosper." This manner enraged King Ahab, and he demanded the truth. Then the expression of Micaiah's face underwent a change; and he spoke out with indescribable solemnity:

I saw all Israel scattered upon the hills, as sheep that have not a shepherd: and the Lord said, These have no master: let them return every man to his house in peace.

Ahab turned to his royal colleague, and cried angrily, "What did I tell you?" But before Jehoshaphat had time to speak, the face of Micaiah took on a rapt expression, like the countenance of a man who sees a strange vision. His mind was distant from the kings and the prophets there assembled; he regarded neither the time nor the place; he saw Jehovah the King of kings seated on the throne of heaven, with the angelic hosts before him:

And the Lord said, Who shall persuade Ahab, that he may go up and fall at Ramoth-Gilead? And one said on this manner, and another said on that manner.

And there came forth a spirit, and stood before the Lord, and said, I will persuade him. ... I will go forth, and I will be a lying spirit in the mouth of all his prophets.

Zedekiah's professional pride was sorely hurt by this utterance; his iron horns grew hot in his hands; he rushed at Micaiah, struck him fiercely in the face, and said scornfully, "Which way went the Spirit of the Lord from me to speak unto thee?" and Micaiah, unmoved both by insult and by blow, responded gravely, "Behold, thou shalt see in that day, when thou shalt go into an inner chamber to hide thyself."

King Ahab prorogued the assembly by commanding that Micaiah be thrown into a dungeon, and fed on miserable rations, until he should return in triumph. But Micaiah told him that he should not return at all, and called all the audience to witness.

What the good Jehoshaphat thought of this extraordinary scene, we shall never know; but he not only consented to enter the battle, he agreed to disguise himself in Ahab's uniform; he was indeed amiable.

Now the King of Syria was out for big game; and he commanded all his captains to pay no attention to anybody except the King of Israel. Therefore when they saw Jehoshaphat in his chariot, the tide of battle turned that way; and the King of Judah cried out, in desperate peril. The Syrians, seeing he was not their man, turned aside; but an unknown archer, taking a mere chance, shot into the host of Israel, and hit Ahab between the joints of his armour; Ahab told the driver to drive to the rear, for he was wounded. Friends supported him all day, so that his condition could not be known by his army; the dying man sat straight in his chariot. The victory was won by the Syrians, and the command to the retreating Hebrews was for a complete dispersion, every man to his home, in accordance with the vision of Micaiah.

King Ahab died at sunset, and as the servants were washing the chariot by the pool of Samaria, stray dogs appeared, who licked up the royal blood, even as Elijah had foretold in the pleasant garden of Naboth.

Ahab was succeeded on the throne of Israel by his son Ahaziah, who followed his father and mother in doing evil continually. It is interesting to observe how much better the kings of Judah behaved than the kings of Israel. The criminal conduct of Jeroboam was a pattern for his followers.

The last hours of Elijah were at hand; but before his dramatic exit, he spoke terrible words and did terrible things. King Ahaziah fell through a window, and was confined to his bed; he enquired of a pagan god whether he should recover. But the messengers he sent on this mission were encountered on the highway by Elijah, who told them to turn back and tell the king that the only true God declared that he should never leave his bed alive. Ahaziah asked the thoroughly frightened emissaries as to the appearance and manner of the man who spoke to them, and they said, "It was an hairy man, and girt with a girdle of leather about his loins." And the king said, "It is Elijah the Tishbite."

Accordingly Ahaziah sent a captain and fifty men to capture the prophet; and when this unfortunate company drew near their destination, they saw the lonely prophet sitting on a throne of his own; sitting on the top of a little hill. The captain, who seems to have done only his duty, spoke with sufficient respect, saying, "Thou man of God, the king hath said, 'Come down.'" Elijah's answer was a blast of flame from heaven, which devoured the whole company. A second captain was sent out, and he bravely gave the same message, adding adverbially, "Come down quickly." He was greeted by the same fiery answer, which consumed him and his soldiers. A third captain was sent out, and he had learned something by the fate of his predecessors; for although he had been accustomed to command, he saw that he had to do with an exceptional case, and he thought there had been enough playing with fire. He left his fifty men at the foot of the hill, while he, with what terror may be imagined, went up alone to the prophet, fell on his knees, and entreated him: "O man of God, I pray thee, let my life, and the life of these fifty thy servants, be precious in thy sight." Elijah's anger was turned away by this soft question, and he accompanied the men of war to the king's palace. He went into the bedchamber, and told Ahaziah to his face that he should surely die. And Ahaziah died.

Seldom has anyone shown such eagerness to receive bad news in person; but Ahaziah was a king, and had the obstinacy that so often accompanies density of mind.

Elijah himself had never been afraid of fire. It was his element. With it he had demonstrated his religion against the prophets of Baal, with it he had annihilated one hundred and two military men, and it was therefore natural that he should depart in a flaming chariot. Accompanied by his heir, Elisha, who was to perform many more miracles than he, the stern old man drew near to Bethel, where Jacob had wrestled with the angel. There the divinity students came out and whispered to Elisha, "Knowest thou that the Lord will take away thy master from thy head today?" And he told them tartly that the question was unnecessary. Elijah tested his companion by repeatedly asking him to cease following him; but Elisha, who never lacked assurance, knew that great things were to happen, and that the day would be forever memorable. He refused to depart, and clung to the side of his teacher. When they got to Jericho, the divinity students came out and asked the same question heard at Bethel; and Elisha made the same rejoinder. Fifty of them followed curiously afar off, for wonders were in the air. The two prophets stood on the bank of Jordan; Elijah took his stiff mantle, rolled it up like a staff, and smote the waters, which receded on both sides, and the pair walked over on solid ground. Then Elijah turned to the persevering Elisha, and told him he was about to be taken away. Was there any particular request Elisha had in mind? Immediately Elisha demanded boldly, "Let a double portion of thy spirit be upon me." Elijah was amazed at the audacity of the petition, but he replied after a moment's thought, that if Elisha should see him in his departure, he would then know that his heart's desire would be fulfilled. Nothing can exceed the majesty of the language that describes the following scene:

And it came to pass, as they still went on, and talked, that, behold, there appeared a chariot of fire, and horses of fire, and parted them both asunder; and Elijah went up by a whirlwind into heaven. And Elisha saw it, and he cried, My father, my father, the chariot of Israel, and the horsemen thereof. And he saw him no more: and he took hold of his own clothes, and rent them in two pieces.

Amid the flaming tempest of Elijah's ascension, a dark object came whirling through the air, and fell to the ground; Elisha seized upon it, and took possession. It was the mantle of the departed prophet, and his successor then knew that he was inspired with a double portion of the spirit that had animated the old hero, and given him power to perform many mighty works. The mantle of Elijah had fallen upon Elisha.

Elijah is one of the most famous among the sons of men. His character is more sublime than lovable; for it was his destiny to be a steadfast servant of God among many apostates, and to speak the truth when it was most unwelcome. He is a dark and tragic figure, outlined against a gay and pleasure-loving court; his loneliness is most appealing; and indeed those who devote themselves in all sincerity to the Divine Will must have souls capable of withstanding the terrors of solitude. They must make their own world, for they do not share the common aims of society. Yet their darkness is lightened by the lamp of the Holy Spirit.

From the literary point of view, the personality of Elijah is of the very essence of romance; he had fallen on evil days, and his menacing face and voice appearing and sounding when most unexpected, have that element of contrast that belongs most particularly to great drama.

VIII

THE PROPHET ELISHA

His Selection by Elijah—Immense Influence of Elisha —His Numerous Miracles—His Vitality—His Leaving His Father and Mother—His Youthful Modesty Hardening Into the Pride of Office—Dangers of Ecclesiastical Snobbery—The Purifying of the City Water Plant at Jericho—Elisha's Cruelty in Murdering Little Children—The War with Moab—The Three Kings—War's Destruction—Tine Widow's Debt—Hospitality of a Prominent Society Woman—The Pleasant Study and Bedroom of Elisha—His Restoration of the Sun-struck Boy—Browning's Allusion—Story of Naaman—Religious Etiquette—Fate of Gehazi—Raising of the Axe—Imponderable Allies in Battle—The Famine at the Siege—Degradation and Approaching Destruction of Israel—Elisha's Brand of Patriotism— His Weeping—Hazael the Dog—The Revolution of Jehu—Assassination of Two Kings—Defiant Jezebel— Bloody Days—Athaliah and the New King—The Arrow at the Window—Death of Elisha—His Influence.

Four years before the death of King Ahab, Elijah appointed Elisha, the son of Shaphat, to be his successor; until the translation of the prophet, the younger man acted as a kind of private secretary and body-servant, accompanying the man of God on his pilgrimages hither and thither; but after the flaming exit of his master, Elisha became Prophet of Israel and held this exalted and dangerous post fifty-five years. He is one of the grandest figures in Hebrew history. His importance and influence are marked by the extraordinary number of miracles he performed; his career was filled with amazing adventures. He must have found life tremendously interesting, for there was scarcely a day without excitement. Although his personality lacks the romantic gloom enveloping the lonely figure of Elijah, the disciple became more powerful than his teacher, exerting a deep influence on both Israelites and aliens. He kept the faith with unswerving passion; the consciousness of his divine mission was so paramount that he spoke to kings and nobles as a plenipotentiary speaks to a vassal.

The name Elisha means *God is Saviour*. During his life he saved many, and his vitality was so astounding that even after his death and burial, his dry bones had more force than radium.

Seldom has so distinguished a career been told in so few words; the sayings and deeds of Elisha are immortal both in literature and in their moral influence; yet his entire biography covers only a dozen chapters in the Bible.

The first meeting of Elijah and Elisha is charming. The former had left the cave where he had listened to the still small voice, and had walked directly to a great farm. There he found Elisha, the son of Shaphat, plowing with twelve yoke of oxen before him, and he with the twelfth. Does this mean that the young man was driving twenty-four oxen in pairs before the plow? If so, he must have been a more skillful driver than Ben-Hur, and the soil must have been tougher than the Puritans found in New England.

However this may be, Elijah silently cast his mantle upon him, significant of the day of wonder when he should receive it in perpetuity; Elisha knew instantly that his work as a farmer had ended forever. But he was an affectionate son; he ran after the man of God, and said, "Let me, I pray thee, kiss my father and my mother, and then I will follow thee." Elijah must have smiled, perhaps for the only time in his life. He looked on the young man and loved him, and answered softly, "Go back again: for what have I done to thee?" Elisha ran to the farmhouse, kissed old Shaphat and his wife, hurried back to where Elijah was waiting, slew two oxen, built a fire with the wooden harness, and there was a solemn farewell feast, in which the family and all the farm-hands participated. Then Elisha followed Elijah, and ministered unto him, leaving Shaphat solitary but proud—proud as only a religious old farmer can be, when his son becomes a clergyman.

It is perhaps unfortunate that the sweet and unaffected humility which characterised the young Elisha should have left him on his assumption of office. But such is the way of all flesh; the frank young prince may become the domineering king; the humble priest may become the haughty cardinal; the unassuming parson may grow into the arrogant bishop. Not even God's holy servants can all stand prosperity; but are to their own past as the Trust Magnate is to his distant clerkship. Early modesty sometimes disappears in the pride of office and the smother of flattery accompanying it. Some golden-hearted village preachers become ecclesiastical snobs. It is especially necessary that all professional religious teachers should pray every day, *Lead us not into temptation.*

Whatever may be the necessity or the desirability in hierarchical forms of religion, I think it is fortunate that the ordinary Christian minister has lost the social prestige and authority that formerly enveloped his person. It is well that there should be respect toward the Servants of God, as toward the Servants of the Nation; but the respect should be to the man rather than to the office. In

Puritan days, the minister walked the street as a captain treads the quarter-deck; people doffed their hats, and spoke to him with deference. I am sure this was not always good for these religious chieftains. Pride establishes an insuperable barrier between human hearts. If I were a minister, I should feel insulted if men changed their ordinary conversation as I entered the room; or if on the train some commercial traveller swore, adding, "Beg your pardon, parson," as if I were a woman. As in the days of chivalry, such thin courtesy fails to conceal the real contempt. It is impossible that all men who hold high office in the church should, in the beauty of their character, equal the marvellous bishop in *Les Misérables,* who yet was drawn from the life; but there is no greater tragedy than by becoming a leader to cease being a Christian.

Have we misjudged here, over-armed our knight,
Given gold and silk where plain hard steel serves best,
Enfeebled whom we sought to fortify,
Made an archbishop and undone a saint?

As soon as the last trace of flame that marked the ascending Elijah had vanished from the sky, Elisha seized the mantle, and returned toward the river Jordan. As he stood on the edge of the flowing stream, he cried out, "Where is the Lord God of Elijah?" Suiting the action to the word, he smote the water with Elijah's mantle; a dry lane appeared, and Elisha crossed to the opposite bank. The same divinity students of Jericho that had watched the two prophets with such curiosity, now saw the younger man returning alone. They came up to him, bowed to the ground, and made a singular request. Fifty of them were athletes, and asked permission to go and search for Elijah, "lest per-adventure the Spirit of the Lord hath taken him up, and cast him upon some mountain, or into some valley." Elisha naturally refused; but their continued pertinacity made him ashamed, and he finally granted the desired permission. Fifty of them eagerly departed on the trail; how they crossed Jordan we do not know; but their expedition was fruitless, and they returned rather crestfallen to Jericho, where Elisha had waited for them. He said, "I told you so."

His confidence in his miraculous powers, established by the separation of the waters of Jordan, was further increased at Jericho. The citizens called his attention to the fact that the city water supply had become contaminated, so that frequent deaths resulted. Elisha ordered them to bring him a new, clean vessel, and to put salt in it. With this in his hand, he went to the reservoir, threw in the salt, and declared the water healed. It has been pure ever since.

Immediately after this good work of sanitation came the event which has left on the character of Elisha an ineffaceable stain. Elijah was a hairy man, but Elisha, although he was young, was noticeably bald; and, like many who have lost their hair, "was sensitive. As he drew near to the town of Bethel, swelling with the new grandeur of his office, feeling his prophetic oats, a covey of little children came flying toward him, and instead of being overawed by his dignity, they were amused by his premature baldness—trust them for noting any peculiarity! They mocked him, and shouted, "Go up, thou bald head; go up, thou bald head."

These children are the same in all places and all times; they are the children of the streets, the newsboys, gamins, sharp-eyed waifs. The muckers of the city of Bethel were in nowise different from the muckers of Paris, London, or Chicago; they saluted Elisha in the same derisory fashion as greets any rather pompous pedestrian. Elisha, alas, had no sense of humour, and a dreadful thing happened. He turned back and cursed them loudly; and before the echoes of his cursing had died on the air, two she-bears came out of a thicket, and tore forty-two children. It is not recorded that the prophet felt any remorse; at that moment he was more like the wild beasts than like a little child.

In no justification of this abominable deed, but as an explanation of his uncompromising severity, it should be remembered that the prophet Elisha lived in days of apostasy and sin; all around him he saw a decadent and corrupt society, that had cynically turned its back on both God and morality. He was a voice of truth in an age of error. The times were evil. Idolatry and sensuality were rampant, and every hour brought nearer the shadow of Assyria.

Jehoram succeeded his father Ahab on the throne of Israel; he was an improvement, for he put away the image of Baal; but he followed Jeroboam in the ways of darkness. The subjected king of Moab had paid a mighty tribute of provisions to Israel, sending regularly a hundred thousand lambs and a hundred thousand unsheared rams. But after the defeat and death of Ahab, he thought it safe to stop these payments. Accordingly, Jehoram collected an army for a punitive expedition. He sent to the worthy Jehoshaphat, king of Judah, whose advancing years had not lessened his extraordinary amiability. Jehoshaphat made the same reply that he had formerly made to Ahab, "I am as thou art, my people as thy people, and my horses as thy horses." With the monarch of Edom as ally, the three kings advanced with their armies. But there was no water, and Jehoram was in despair. Jehoshaphat reminded him, as he had reminded his father, that it might be well to take counsel of a prophet of the Lord. It is perhaps natural that the name of Elisha should have been better known to the servants of the king than to the king himself; at all events, one of Jehoram's servants suggested that the famous successor of the famous Elijah was within reach; and the good Jehoshaphat said delightedly, "The word of the Lord is with him."

It is an interesting and significant fact, that instead of sending for Elisha, the three kings paid him a visit in person. Their reception was anything but respectful. Elisha glared at Jehoram, and in the most insulting tone recommended him to consult the prophets of his father and mother. The king of Israel must have been very thirsty, for instead of resenting this language he begged Elisha to help them, saying they were in deadly peril. Elisha looked at the benevolent countenance of the good king of Judah and said sternly, "Were it not that I regard the presence of Jehoshaphat the king of Judah, I would not look toward thee, nor see thee."

Then Elisha called for a minstrel; and as the minstrel played ravishing music, he was inspired. He told them to make many ditches, for although there would come neither wind nor rain, water would flood the valley, so that there would be more than sufficient for man and beast. The Moabites would be delivered into their hands, and they should show no mercy.

Next morning, indeed, the valley shone with water, and to the disordered eyes of the Moabite host it looked like blood. They believed that the three kings had fought with one another; "now, therefore, Moab, to the spoil." Unfortunately for them, they found a united and grimly determined host, who slaughtered them relentlessly. The Israelites pursued the shrieking fugitives into their own country. They killed all the men, women, and children ; they stopped all the wells of water; they felled all the good trees; they ruined every piece of profitable land.

War is always horrible. No nation in ancient or modern times suffered worse than those who were defeated by the children of Israel; the method was annihilation, which spared neither women, nor children, nor farms, nor temples; they were meaning to make their foes permanently helpless. It is not at all surprising that we find the Bible historian commenting on the feelings of the defeated Moabites in this fashion: "And there was great indignation against Israel." What savages, they must have reflected, were the chosen people!

We forget how destructive war is till we live under its curse. One reason why the recent great war had such a novel air of horrible wickedness is because people for the most part do not read history; apart from the devilish inventions of science, the same things happened in our time that have so often followed the track of war—slaughter, destruction of orchards and crops, sickness, famine, and the high cost of living.

A certain widow came to Elisha, and told a story in which the woe of a million defenceless widows is revealed. In the permanent absence of the man of the house, the cruel creditor descended upon the lone woman, and threatened to take away for payment of debt the only property she had. This consisted of her two sons, who were to be seized. Elisha asked her what she had in the house. It appeared that the poor creature had nothing except one pot of oil. He accordingly told her to borrow "not a few" empty vessels of her neighbours, to retire into the house with her sons, to shut the door, and then to pour oil into the numerous receptacles. This she did until all were filled. She was then informed that she must sell the oil, pay the debt, and live in security on what remained. I wish I could have seen the countenance of her creditor when she paid him in cash as hard as his face.

Cultivated and fashionable women have often received spiritual leaders with enthusiasm. One day, when Elisha was in Shunem, he met a prominent society woman; she was impressed, and invited the prophet to dinner. Thereafter, whenever he happened to visit the town, he accepted her standing invitation, and always stopped at her house. In view of the frequency of these journeys, she suggested to her husband that they make a slight addition to the house, consisting of a new room on the roof, that should be for the exclusive use of Elisha, where he could keep what things he needed, and always feel at home. This was done; a room was built, and furnished with a bed, a table, a chair, and a candlestick; it must have been exceedingly attractive in its quiet seclusion; there the prophet could study, think, and have repose. He was naturally grateful, and on one occasion he told his servant Gehazi to call the lady of the house, and she soon stood before him. He reminded her of all her graceful hospitality, and asked what he might do for her in return. Would she like to be recommended to the king or to the commander-in-chief? But she replied that she was contented to dwell in her household with her numerous friends. The prophet was at a loss, but as soon as she had left the room Gehazi, who never lacked assurance, suggested that she was childless and perhaps lonely, as her husband was an old man. Elisha had her recalled, and as she stood in the doorway he gave her the amazing news that in one year hence she should hold a baby boy in her arms. Like Abraham, she thought this was a pleasantry and was not altogether appreciative; but the next year she had her son.

When he was about six years old, he went out to the wheat-field on a day of fierce heat. Suddenly he cried out to his father, "My head! My head!" His father had him taken home immediately and his mother held him in her arms until noon, when he died. In her desperate anguish, she thought on the man of God, and believed in his power even over the grave. She carried the body up to the guest room, laid it on the bed, asked her husband to send to her immediately one of the young men, and to have an ass saddled, that she might hurry to Elisha.

She mounted the ass, bade the young servant drive and run alongside as fast as possible, and after a time they appeared before the man of God. But he had seen her while she was yet a great way off. He sent Gehazi to meet her, and to enquire after the health of the family. Perhaps no greater instance of faith is recorded than in her answer. Gehazi asked, "Is it well with the child?" She answered, "It is well."

Then she fell before Elisha, and clasped his feet; and when Gehazi roughly tried to drag her away, the prophet commanded to let her alone, for her distress was evident. She breathed out some incoherent remark about her son, and Elisha told Gehazi to take his staff and run straight to the lady's house, saluting no man on the way, and there to place the staff on the face of the child. But this did not suit the mother at all; she wanted the specialist, not his assistant; so Elisha himself had to go back with her. Gehazi did as he was told and, meeting the prophet on his way, the servant said ironically, "The child is not awaked."

The man of God went into the room and shut the door. He prayed; he covered the child with his own warm body, mouth to mouth and eyes to eyes. The rigid little form grew flexible, the child sneezed seven times, opened his eyes, and looked around in bewilderment. Elisha called for Gehazi, and told him to fetch the mother. As soon as she entered the room, he said calmly, "Take up thy son." She bowed down in rapture, fell at the feet of the man of God, and carried away her boy in triumph.

In *The Ring and the Book,* Browning makes a striking reference to this incident; he is speaking of his own recreation of a story, long dead, which now is made to live again by the creative power of imagination:

    Was not Elisha once—
Who bade them lay his staff on a corpse-face?
There was no voice, no hearing: he went in,
Therefore, and shut the door upon them twain,
And prayed unto the Lord: and he went up
And lay upon the corpse, dead on the couch,
And put his mouth upon its mouth, his eyes
Upon its eyes, his hands upon its hands,
And stretched him on the flesh;the flesh waxed warm;
And he returned, walked to and fro the house,
And went up, stretched him on the flesh again,
And the eyes opened. 'Tis a credible feat
With the right man and way.

One day at Gilgal, while the sons of the prophets were sitting at his feet and listening to his talk, he commanded Gehazi to set a great pot on the fire and boil herbs for a repast. One went out into the fields to gather and unknowingly put poisonous wild gourds into the pot. As they were eating, they felt sharp pains and cried, "O thou man of God, there is death in the pot." But he told them to bring meal, and Elisha cast it into the stew, after which they ate with security. Their faith in him equalled his own powers.

The story of Naaman is one of the most attractive in the Bible, though it has a tragic conclusion. Naaman was commander-in-chief of the Syrian forces, and a favourite of the king, because of his ability, wisdom, and valour; but he was cursed with leprosy. A little Jewish maid, brought to the court as a captive, was in attendance on Naaman's wife, and one day as she was brushing the hair of her mistress she became garrulous and prattled about the leprosy and how she knew a great doctor in Samaria who could cure it. The story came to the ears of the Syrian monarch, who sent Naaman to the king of Israel, with magnificent gifts and a letter which requested the monarch to cure Naaman. The king of Israel was both surprised and dismayed when he read this letter. He tore his clothes; he shrieked, "Am I God, to kill and to make alive? The purpose of this letter is to pick a quarrel." But Elisha, hearing of what had happened, sent word to the king that there was no cause for distress, and suggested that Naaman come in person and he would learn something to his advantage.

Accordingly, the mighty Naaman, with his horses and his chariots and his splendid retinue, came and stood before the portal of Elisha's house, like a modern millionaire coming to a specialist. Elisha did not trouble himself to come to the door or to look out of the window, but sent Gehazi to tell Naaman to go and bathe seven times in the river Jordan. Naaman was not accustomed to take orders from anyone except the king of Syria; his pride had already been irritated by being passed along from the king of Israel to someone else; he had at least supposed that the doctor would come out and perform solemn and mystic rites. Furthermore, what was the tiny stream of Jordan compared to the broad rivers of Damascus? He turned away in a rage.

Then one of his servants—Naaman was certainly fortunate in his servants—taking his courage in both hands, mildly suggested that if the prophet had bade him go through some long and tiresome regimen, he would have obeyed; how much better merely to wash and be clean. Naaman was impressed. He went to the banks of Jordan, and dipped six times with no result. How sceptically, how hopelessly he must have plunged in the seventh time! But to his amazement his hot, dry, diseased skin changed into the fresh, soft, clear skin of a little child, and he was clean. With what unspeakable delight he came up out of the water!

With all his followers he returned to the house of the man of God and Elisha looked upon him graciously. Naaman said exactly the thing the prophet hoped he would say: "Now I know that there is no God in all the earth but in Israel." Then he naturally tried to induce Elisha to accept a fee, which was firmly refused, though Naaman was very persistent. Finally, he asked for a load of earth to take back to Syria, for he meant henceforth to worship

Jehovah, and to offer burnt offerings on this hallowed soil.

Naaman was a gentleman and did not wish to fail in his loyalty to his king, though he had quite ceased to believe in his country's religion. He therefore put a delicate question of religious etiquette before Elisha. It appeared that when the king went into the house of Rimmon to worship, he always leaned on the arm of Naaman, and they bowed down together before the god. Naaman explained that he himself could not now believe in this worship, but that he did not want to make an unpleasant scene. Would it be proper, therefore, for him to show formal respect in the house of Rimmon by bowing the knee, while in his heart remaining faithful to Jehovah? Elisha showed both common sense and courtesy in instantly reassuring the honest warrior— "Go in peace."

(It was good advice. If I were in a temple of Buddha, or in a place of Mohammedan worship, I hope I should show the proper respect and reverence, though Buddha and Mohammed are no more divine to me than Thor or Apollo.)

The pretty story of Naaman does not have a happy ending. The horror of its close takes us unawares. Gehazi had been a silent spectator of Naa-man's offer of reward and his master's refusal; what an idiot to let such an opportunity pass! He followed after the chariot of Naaman; the mighty man alighted in rare good humour and asked if there was anything he could do. Gehazi said that two divinity students had just called on Elisha, and that his master would be pleased if Naaman would send back some money and clothing for them. It was a skilful lie, and the Syrian, only too delighted to show his gratitude, gave Gehazi double what he asked. The servant hid the stolen goods, and stood before his master, who asked sternly where he had been. Gehazi said he had not gone out. Elisha informed him that he had seen the whole transaction as clearly in his mind as if he had been present in person. "Now, Gehazi, you are rich, and can buy all manner of real and personal property, and can have servants to do your bidding. But the leprosy that has left Naaman shall abide with you and your descendants forever." Gehazi said not a word; the pallor of fright blanched into the horrible pallor of disease. And he went out from his presence a leper as white as snow.

I do not think any man, woman, or child has ever read that tragic sentence without terror.

Not only did Elisha perform great miracles, such as bringing the dead back from their slumber, and miracles on a large scale, dealing with vast numbers, but he was not averse to the employment of his powers for any little deed of kindness. Perhaps constant exercise was necessary, and it was important to keep in practice. Once upon a time the divinity students came to him and said that the theological building which they occupied had become too small for their needs. They requested permission to go to the banks of the Jordan, cut down timber, and build there a substantial and spacious dormitory. He consented and even accompanied them thither. As one of the young men was felling a beam, he hit with all his might, and the axe-head flew off the handle and into the river. He cried out in dismay, for he had borrowed the axe, and probably could not afford to buy another. Elisha asked him to point out the exact place where the metal had sunk in the stream; then the prophet took a stick, tossed it on the water, and the iron head of the axe rose like a trout to a fly. The young man reached out and secured it, with what surprise and pleasure may be easily imagined.

Elisha was worth more to the king of Israel in war-time than a thousand generals; for whenever the Syrians planned an ambush or a night attack, the seer, by an admirable system of mind-reading, revealed everything to the king. Naturally the king of Syria believed there was a traitor in his own camp, and he made strenuous efforts to discover his identity. But one of his courtiers, who knew the common gossip, told him that when he lay in bed thinking, his thoughts were revealed to the king of Israel by Elisha. Spies were sent out, who brought back word that the man of God was in Dothan. Accordingly in the night a whole division was sent against the town; and in the morning light, when Elisha and his servant walked forth, they saw the city encompassed with horses and chariots and armed men. The servant trembled, and said: "Alas, my master, what shall we do?" The answer came with calm assurance: "Fear not: for they that be with us are more than they that be with them." All the imponderable forces were on the side of the man of God, but it was natural that the young attendant could not see them. Those who are close to God undoubtedly see visions that are completely out of the range of the children of this world. Spiritual realities are sometimes hidden even from the wise and prudent; but they are nevertheless there. Elisha prayed that the young man might for once see what he himself saw; and to his astonished gaze the mountains were full of horses and chariots of fire, round about, compared to which the glittering host of the Syrians was both dull and puny. As the servant's eyes were opened, the eyes of the Syrians were blinded; so that Elisha walked boldly to their leaders, told them that he would bring them directly to the man they sought, and he did; he led them into the heart of the city of Samaria; there they received sight, and to their bewilderment found themselves in the enemy's capital. The king of Israel hated to let such a chance slip, and said eagerly to Elisha, "My father, shall I smite them? Shall I smite them?" But Elisha refused to allow such treachery; instead of smiting them, he bade the Israelites give them a fine dinner, and they returned to their king with the amazing story. The result was a long peace.

What a pity that this method has not been more frequently adopted! To receive an enemy with hospitable kindness is to disarm him. How the soldiers of the two hostile camps must have fraternised as the food and drink were served! If invading hosts could be invited to dinner, it is possible that much loss and suffering could be averted. If thine enemy hunger, feed him. Plain common sense.

Later, Benhadad, the king of Syria, laid siege to Samaria, with the result that has been so often repeated in history. The price of provisions rose to such a height that a little dung was sold for much silver, and unnatural tragedies became common. As the king of Israel was walking along the wall, a woman cried out for justice. It appeared that she and another woman had compacted to eat their babies; she had boiled hers in good faith; both had shared in the repast; and now the other woman would not play fair, and had hidden her son. When the king heard this dreadful story, which excited the attention of a listening crowd, he tore his clothes in horror and despair; and as the people gazed at his parted garments they saw that he was wearing sackcloth next his skin.

Suddenly the king thought of Elisha, and in his frenzy he determined to kill him, for he believed that all this suffering came from Jehovah. He sent a messenger to Elisha's house, and followed hard after. Now Elisha was sitting within, surrounded by the elders; he told them that they would soon hear the murderer's knock on the door, but not to let him in until the king appeared. Close behind the servant came the king himself, leaning on the arm of a noble; but before the king could open his mouth, Elisha predicted that the next day rich and plenteous provisions would be sold cheaply in the very gate of Samaria, a peck of fine meal for a piece of silver and two pecks of barley for the same price. Unfortunately for his future welfare, the lord accompanying the king sneered, and suggested that if Jehovah would conveniently provide windows in heaven, this event might come to pass. Elisha looked at him coldly and replied, "Thou shalt see it with thine eyes, but shalt not eat thereof."

Four lepers outside the gate took counsel together, and seeing no hope within or without the city, and being in that reckless state of mind that is sometimes characteristic of those suffering from an incurable disease, hit upon the wild plan of going directly into the enemy's camp and asking for food, for the bitterness of death was past. There they found signs of a panic; the Syrians had imagined that they heard the noise of advancing armies, and had fled in such confusion as to leave provisions and jewels in abundance. This was a great night for the lepers, the best the poor wretches had ever known; they feasted prodigiously, hid costly gems, and then returned to the gates of Samaria before dawn and roused the porters. There was a mad rush to the Syrian camp, and as the sceptical lord happened to have charge of the gate, the mob in their wild fury for food rushed right over him; he was trodden under foot, and died, according to the word of the prophet.

The last days of Elisha were clouded by the ruin of Israel, which he knew to be imminent; foreign conquest and civil war were both to devastate the land.

It should be remembered again that it was Judah, and not Israel, that kept alive the Mosaic law and the true Hebrew religion; the northern tribes of Israel were apostate, and under the leadership of their abominable kings, following in the wake of Jeroboam, and led wholly astray by Ahab, from whose rule the country never recovered, their apostasy became so general that the true faith was almost extinguished. When we speak of the Hebrew religion as it has come down to us, we really mean *Judaism,* Jerusalem lasted longer than Israel, but succumbed to Assyria at last.

The history of Israel, beginning with the reign of Ahab, is worse than a decline; it is symbolised by a rudderless boat on a rushing river, running toward irretrievable disaster with constantly accelerating speed until the roar of the drowning cataract is heard.

Elisha saw this as plainly as if it had already happened, and his heart died in his breast; for he loved his country. He loved his country with a love unknown to noisy patriots; he spoke bitterly against the national vices and sins, he condemned the government and the rulers; if he had been indifferent to the nation's welfare he would have remained silent. Often those who speak out most strongly against a national policy are filled with a love of their country so much greater than that of jingo orators that their passion for the fatherland is quite beyond the common understanding. This is nevertheless one of the highest forms of patriotism.

Why Elisha journeyed to Damascus we do not know; but there he was, and Benhadad, the king of Syria, confined to his bed with sickness, heard of his presence, and having a wholesome respect for him, sent a messenger with forty camels laden down with gifts, to ask the prophet if he should recover of this disease. The messenger was Hazael, who, like Macbeth, did not dream of the evil in his own heart. Elisha told him that Benhadad would surely die. When Elisha had said this, he gazed into Hazael's face with such steadfast and searching scrutiny that the bold messenger became embarrassed. . Suddenly the man of God burst into tears.

Perhaps no one ever had more self-control than Elisha. This only recorded occasion when he wept unrestrainedly is therefore highly significant. Hazael asked, "Why weepeth my lord?"

Because I know the evil that thou wilt do unto the children of Israel: their strongholds wilt thou set on fire, and their young men wilt thou slay with the sword, and wilt dash their children, and rip up their women with child.

And Hazael said, But what, is thy servant a dog, that he should do this great thing?

How many youths would feel insulted if some one should tell them in advance of all the evil deeds they would perform during their lives! Perhaps their amazement would be greater than their resentment. "What, do you take me for a beast?" The answer is, "Yes: the very things from which you now recoil in horror, and loudly condemn in others, you yourself will do."

Hazael did not know his own mind, having never explored it. The next day, smitten with ambition, he assassinated the sick king by smothering him with a wet cloth, and thus succeeded him on the throne of Syria.

Joram, the son of Ahab, was king of Israel; he fought against Hazael, lost the battle, was grievously wounded, and returned to Jezreel to recover. There he was visited by Ahaziah, king of Judah. Elisha sent a divinity student to Captain Jehu, telling him to anoint the captain as king of Israel; then to open the door and run away as fast as his legs could carry him. Jehu was at mess with the other officers, and they were naturally curious when the excited messenger sought a private interview with him. No sooner had he returned to the room than they asked him, "Wherefore came this mad fellow to thee?" Captain Jehu told them the truth; with one accord they rallied around him, blew trumpets, and announced the revolution.

Jehu was a man of war—hardy, resolute, and impetuous as fire. He was known everywhere for his daring adventures, and for his reckless driving. As his chariot drew near to the walls of Jezreel, in which city were the two kings of Israel and Judah, he was seen afar off by the watchman on the tower. By the order of King Joram, first one messenger and then another were sent out; but they did not return. By this time the approaching chariot was very near, and the watchman said to his king, "The driving is like the driving of Jehu the son of Nimshi; for he driveth furiously."

Then Joram knew his hour had struck; both he and Ahaziah went out to meet the captain, and they encountered him in that very garden of Naboth which Joram's father had stolen. When they came within earshot Joram cried, "Is it peace, Jehu?" and Jehu replied by calling his mother Jezebel a vile name. Joram wheeled his chariot about, to escape; but Jehu drew a bow with his full strength, the arrow transfixed Joram, and he died in the portion of land that had been stolen from Naboth.

Then Ahaziah fled by way of the garden house, but Jehu was out king-hunting that day, and the retreating monarch of Judah was slain in his chariot.

Long ago, Elijah had foretold the death of Jezebel; she had survived her husband, had now lived to see her son assassinated, and knew that she and the whole race of Ahab were to be exterminated. But it is impossible to withhold admiration for the manner in which this iron-hearted queen met her fate. She had been the wife of Ahab, and was the daughter of a king. She was high-bred, and showed no fear, but only defiance, as the revolutionary chieftain approached. She painted her face and adorned her head, as if for a state occasion, and looked out from an upper window. As Jehu, flushed with tasting blood, entered the palace yard, she greeted him with a taunt, reminding him that he was nothing but a traitor and a foul cutthroat. Jehu called aloud; some servants looked out of the windows, and Jehu commanded them to throw her down. She was hurled to the ground, and Jehu drove furiously over her prostrate body. He then went in to eat, but looking up from the table, he gave orders to bury the accursed woman, "for she is a king's daughter." The attendants found nothing but a few bones; the dogs had already devoured her, as had been long since foretold by Elijah the Tishbite.

Jehu was not satisfied with having killed two kings and a queen in one expedition; he sent word to Samaria, and had the heads of Ahab's seventy sons, every head in a separate basket, brought to him. He then gave orders which resulted in the destruction of every relative of Ahab's family, so that the whole house perished from the earth. These were bloody days. Jehu was determined to clean house and after he had slaughtered every relative and servant of Ahab, he killed all the priests of Baal and turned their temple into a public convenience.

Yet, after all this holy zeal, King Jehu departed from the worship of Jehovah and set up a golden calf. He was like average humanity in being part good and part evil; the reign of this man of violence lasted twenty-eight years, and he died in his bed.

After the death of Ahaziah, king of Judah, who was killed by Jehu, his mother Athaliah—a desperately wicked woman—slew all the seed royal, except Jehoash, who was hidden by his aunt. Athaliah reigned six years, thinking she was secure; when one day young Jehoash was suddenly brought out in public and crowned by Jehoiada the priest. The people clapped their hands and shouted, God save the king! Athaliah heard the sound of the trumpets and the voices of the multitude, and came out of the palace, where, to her amazement, she saw her living grandson receiving public homage. Athaliah rent her clothes and cried *Treason, Treason*—but those were her last words, and Jehoash became king of Judah.

Racine wrote a play about this royal adventuress, as he did of Esther; but even his genius failed to equal in force the language of the Bible.

Jehoahaz the son of Jehu succeeded his father on the throne of Israel, and was constantly humiliated by the victorious Hazael, king of Syria, so that only a remnant of power was left to the nation. It was during the reign of Joash, the son of Jehoahaz, that Elisha fell into his last sickness. He was old and full of honours, universally respected; King Joash paid a visit in person to his bedside. When he entered the room and saw the once haughty prophet lying helpless on his bed, the king wept and repeated the words that Elisha had cried out to the departing Elijah: "O my father, my father, the chariot of Israel, and the horsemen thereof!"

The dying prophet commanded the king to take bow and arrows, and fling wide open a window to the east. Then when Joash had drawn back the bowstring, Elisha raised himself up in bed and placed his hand on the hand of the king, and said "Shoot." The arrow flew far away in the direction of the land of Syria, and Elisha told Joash it was a symbol of deliverance from the ever-threatening peril. Then he told the monarch to smite the floor with arrows; and he smote three times and stopped. The old prophet was angry, and said he had stopped too soon; if he had struck five or six times, he would have completely beaten the Syrian forces. Now he should enjoy only three victories.

The prophet's anger has always seemed to me unreasonable; how was the poor king to know the number of times he should smite the floor? But I suppose Elisha meant him to keep on striking until he should hear the command to desist; or perhaps he struck the floor without any conviction, thinking it was just a dying man's whim, and humouring him as we humour those who are very sick. He had cause later to regret it.

Elisha died, and long after his death, when nothing remained of him but dry bones, his skeleton had such vitality that a corpse, being let down into the same grave, happened to touch the dusty remains of the prophet; and to the astonishment of the mourners, the dead man sprang out of the tomb. There was no danger that Elisha would ever be forgotten.

Benjamin Franklin once said, "If the people are as bad as they are with religion, what would they be without it?" Thus, considering how evil the children of Israel were under the constant admonitions, warnings, and mighty deeds of Elisha, what would they have been without his presence? All nations, I suppose, have been destroyed from within; the neglect of religion and morality has set many proud empires on the slope to ruin. Yet even in the darkest days, when doom is certain, there has always been some witness to the power of truth and righteousness ; some man who has not surrendered to the gods of folly and selfishness. Such a tower was the prophet Elisha; he was like a tall lighthouse on a dark night; he blazed out the truth faithfully, and it was not his fault when the ship of state went on the rocks.

IX

THE DOWNFALL OF ISRAEL AND JUDAH

THE PATRIOTIC STORIES OF DANIEL AND ESTHER

Reasons for the Loss of Empires—Social Life in Israel and in Judah—The Good King Hezekiah—The Destruction of Sennacherib—Byron's Poem—Sickness and Prayer of Hezekiah—The Prophet Isaiah—Hezekiah's Magnificent Poem on Life and Death—Louis XV— The Evil Reign of Manasseh—Renaissance of Morality Under the Good Boy Josiah—His Zeal as a Reformer—Last Days of Judah—The Conquest and Captivity—The Brilliant Youth Daniel—His Three Friends—Their Independence—Daniel the First Vegetarian—Daniel the Psycho-analyst—The Mediums— The Dream and Interpretation—The Fiery Furnace— The Three Salamanders—The King Eats Grass—Belshazzar's Feast—The Writing—Daniel and the Den of Lions—Patriotic Emphasis in Daniel and in Esther—Independence of Vashti—Selection of Esther— Proud Mordecai the Jew—The Pompous Haman and His Fate—Insomnia of the King—The Whirligig of Time Brings in His Revenges—Grand Patriotic Conclusion

When the moral law is continually broken, either by individuals, communities, or nations, a false security may last for a time, illusory as sin itself; but sooner or later evil conduct is followed by evil results, as certainly as winter follows autumn. Nations that put their confidence in the gods of iron and steel rather than in the God of Truth and Righteousness, are doomed. Both the Old and the New Testament point out the path of true national glory.

"In God We Trust" is a better national motto than "America First."

The Israelites, who had entered Canaan so proudly under Captain Joshua, who had triumphed repeatedly under King David, were utterly humiliated by Assyria. After a siege of three years, the city of Samaria was taken and the Assyrians carried away the inhabitants into captivity; it is worth remembering, in justice to these heathen, that they treated their conquered foes more humanely than Israel had behaved toward the cities they had overcome. They placed garrisons in many Hebrew towns, and it must have been a strange sight to see the men and women from faraway Babylon dwelling like a superior race in Israel.

The social life of the tribe of Judah was so much better than the standard of morality farther north that Jerusalem was able to keep back the invaders for many years; and if it had not been for one thoroughly bad king, Manasseh, Judah might never have succumbed. Then, as in European history, fashions in character and religion were set by the king.

Everyone who is interested in the welfare of modern Europe and America, everyone who is interested in the welfare of the white race, will find valuable material for thought in reading the Second Book of the Kings. Human nature has not changed, neither has the law of causation. When a nation loses its soul, it becomes vulnerable to foreign attack. Nor is there, from the world point of view, much to regret in the results of such weakness, however regrettable the weakness itself may be. A nation that has lost its soul does not deserve power.

The moral life of the kingdom of Judah fluctuated according to the standards of character followed by her rulers; during the last century before the fall of Jerusalem there were bad kings and good kings. Among the latter, two fine specimens of royalty stand out in bold relief—Hezekiah and the good boy Josiah. The old faith shone brightly again in these two reigns, all the brighter by reason of the following darkness. During the rule of Hezekiah, a prophet arose whose influence on literature and on conduct has been immeasurably powerful. His name is Isaiah.

It was during Hezekiah's reign in Judah that Samaria fell before the Assyrian besiegers, and the kingdom of Israel fell with it. Sennacherib, the king of Assyria, also invaded Judah, and Hezekiah was forced to pay him an enormous indemnity; but later, a successful rebellion was organised and carried through. The Assyrians came down and laid siege to Jerusalem with an immense army, and Rab-shakeh, their emissary, made a long speech, counselling the inhabitants to surrender, because, said he, Sennacherib is invincible. He ridiculed the God of Judah and pointed out to the people what had become of all the other nations who had fought against Assyria and who had trusted in their gods.

This speech of Rabshakeh's is remarkable; it is exactly the kind of talk one so often hears, the talk of the "practical" men in ridicule of ideals. What good will it do you to trust in God if I take away your money and provisions? He was a plain fighting man who believed that if one had superior armaments one was bound to win. Spiritual forces were to him meaningless.

Rabshakeh had learned the Hebrew language, and when he met the diplomats of Hezekiah in front of the walls of Jerusalem, they begged him to talk Aramaic, so that the people on the walls could not hear. They desired secret diplomacy. But the clever Rabshakeh particularly wished the famine-suffering men and women on the walls to hear what he had to say, so he spoke fair words in a loud voice, and in the Hebrew tongue. He advised them not to hearken to Hezekiah, but to rise in revolt, open the gates, and surrender Jerusalem to him, and after a time he would lead them away

to a land like your own land, a land of corn and wine, a land of bread and vineyards, a land of olive oil and of honey, that ye may live and not die: and hearken not unto Hezekiah, when he persuadeth you, saying, The Lord will deliver us.

Hath any of the gods of the nations delivered at all his land out of the hand of the king of Assyria?

Where are the gods of Hamath, and of Arpad? Where are the gods of Sepharvaim, Hena, and Ivah? Have they delivered Samaria out of thine hand? Who are they among all the gods of the countries, that have delivered their country out of mine hand, that the Lord should deliver Jerusalem out of mine hand?

The splendid discipline of the good King Hezekiah is shown in the reception that greeted these fine speeches:

But the people held their peace, and answered him not a word: for the king's commandment was, saying, Answer him not.

Hezekiah took counsel of Isaiah, the man of God, who first appears in history at this crisis; Isaiah bade him be of good courage, for the Assyrians were to be destroyed and the mighty King Sennacherib assassinated. Furthermore, the doom would fall upon them in precisely the manner that would be most convincing, both to them and to Judah, that the Lord God omnipotent reigneth. "I will put my hook in thy nose, and my bridle in thy lips, and I will turn thee back by the way by which thou earnest."

That night one hundred and eighty-five thousand in the Assyrian host were smitten with sudden death. Sennacherib decided that the location was unhealthy and departed to Nineveh, when one fine day, as he was publicly worshipping his particular little god, he was stabbed to death by his own sons.

As everyone ought to know, Byron's lyrical poems called *Hebrew Melodies* are interesting and melodious versions of Old Testament stories. One of the most famous is *The Destruction of Sennacherib*.

The Assyrian came down like the wolf on the fold,
And his cohorts were gleaming in purple and gold;
And the sheen of their spears was like stars on the sea,
When the blue wave rolls nightly on deep Galilee.

Like the leaves of the forest when Summer is green,
The host with their banners at sunset are seen:
Like the leaves of the forest when Autumn hath blown,
That host on the morrow lay wither'd and strown.

For the Angel of Death spread his wings on the blast,
And breathed in the face of the foe as he pass'd;
And the eyes of the sleepers wax'd deadly and chill,
And their hearts but once heav'd, and forever grew still!

In the midst of the pleasures and cares of royal authority, and with his mind full of plans for the civic welfare, Hezekiah fell into a dangerous sickness, so that his life was despaired of; Isaiah came to see him and told him bluntly to set his house in order, for he would not recover. The good king turned his face to the wall and prayed, reminding the Lord of how extremely well he had behaved, and how pious he had been. Then he wept copiously, for never until the day of Dr. Johnson was there a man who loved life with more gusto, or who was more afraid of death. His prayer was so effective that Isaiah was divinely commanded to grant him a reprieve, which should last fifteen years; furthermore, the Assyrian triumph would be postponed until after his death.

When King Hezekiah recovered from his sickness, he wrote the following poem, one of the most beautiful passages in the Bible:

I said in the cutting off of my days, I shall go to the gates of the grave: I am deprived of the residue of my years.
I said, I shall not see the Lord, even the Lord, in the land of the living: I shall behold man no more with the inhabitants of the world.
Mine age is departed, and is removed from me as a shepherd's tent: I have cut off like a weaver my life: he will cut me off with pining sickness: from day even to night wilt thou make an end of me.
I reckoned till morning, that, as a lion, so will he break all my bones: from day even to night wilt thou make an end of me.
Like a crane or a swallow, so did I chatter: I did mourn as a dove: mine eyes fail with looking upward: O Lord, I am oppressed; undertake for me.
What shall I say? He hath both spoken unto me, and himself hath done it: I shall go softly all my years in the bitterness of my soul.
O Lord, by these things men live, and in all these things is the life of my spirit: so wilt thou recover me, and make me to live.
Behold, for peace I had great bitterness: but thou hast in love to my soul

delivered it from the pit of corruption: for thou hast cast all my sins behind my back.
For the grave cannot praise thee, death cannot celebrate thee: they that go down into the pit cannot hope for thy truth.
The living, the living, he shall praise thee, as I do this day: the father of the children shall make known thy truth.
The Lord was ready to save me: therefore we will sing my songs to the stringed instruments all the days of our life in the house of the Lord.

The intense love of life and horror of annihilation expressed so poignantly in this psalm appeared in a less noble fashion when Isaiah stood before the king one day and foretold the destruction of Jerusalem, saying that Hezekiah's own sons should be degraded into slaves in the Assyrian palace. Hezekiah replied with a frank statement of his own selfish love of ease and security, "Good is the word of the Lord, because these things will not come to pass until after I am gone." His reception of Isaiah's prophecy infallibly reminds us of another king, Louis XV, who in strikingly similar circumstances said cynically, "After us the deluge."

Manasseh, the son of Hezekiah, succeeded him on the throne of Judah; he was an unprincipled scoundrel, under whom the nation became so degenerate that its doom was merely a question of date. This man, however, reigned fifty-five years, one of the longest reigns in Bible history, so that, like Louis XIV and Louis XV, he had every opportunity to accomplish the ruin of his country. His son Amon became so impossible that he was assassinated after being two years on the throne, and the "people of the land" took his little boy, Josiah, eight years old, and proclaimed him king. However powerful or cruel the kings were, both in Israel and in Judah, they were never absolute monarchs; democratic sentiment ruled from the time of Saul till the very end; in the last century of the two kingdoms, revolutions and assassinations became so common as to attract only momentary attention.

Josiah was a throw-back to his great-grandfather Hezekiah; he was a thoroughly upright and spiritually minded king, as loyal to Jehovah as David himself. This reign of Josiah is the last brightness before the night of captivity. The sun of Judah, so long in the clouds, emerged just before setting, and shone with a brilliance all the greater because of the coming darkness. Josiah repaired the temple of the Lord, and during the renovation a wonderful thing happened. Hilkiah the High Priest found the book of the Law, which had not only been neglected, but had become as obsolete as statutes quite forgotten. It was like a new revelation, like a reincarnation of Moses himself. When Josiah heard the words of the Law read aloud, he tore his garments; for the contrast between what was and what ought to be was total. He determined to make a thoroughgoing reformation; and first he enquired, curiously enough, of a prophetess named Huldah, who lived in the divinity school in Jerusalem; she received the word of the Lord, which said that Judah was doomed, yet because of the piety and devotion of Josiah, he should not live to see his country made desolate, but should go to his grave in peace.

Instead of complacently rejoicing in this message, as his great-grandfather Hezekiah would have done, he proceeded to do the work of ten men. He knew that the night was coming, and resolved to make the best possible use of his time. He certainly was one of the most admirable characters in monarchical history.

He destroyed every evidence of paganism; he put away the mediums and the abominable fakirs who had enjoyed an ever-increasing authority; he abolished unspeakable but popular practices; he brought back the observances of the Mosaic Law, and they held a Passover Feast which aroused such excitement that the historian says:

Surely there was not holden such a passover from the days of the judges that judged Israel, nor in all the days of the kings of Israel, nor of the kings of Judah...

And like unto him was there no king before him, that turned to the Lord with all his heart, and with all his soul, and with all his might, according to all the law of Moses; neither after him arose there any like him.

This zeal was in part undoubtedly owing to the reaction against previous decadence and sin—a familiar spectacle to all acquainted with history and human nature. But Josiah was in earnest; he may have hoped to turn aside the wrath of the Lord, and thus save Jerusalem. If so, his hopes were vain. All his drastic and heroic operations were palliatives, not remedies; they postponed death, but they did not prevent it. Fortunately for the king, he was killed in battle and was delivered from the evil days. Jehoahaz, his son, was wicked, and was carried off to Egypt in captivity, where he died; his brother Jehoiakim was made king of Judah by Pharaoh, which shows the national degradation; history had repeated itself, and the Hebrews were working to pay taxes and gifts to the Egyptians, just as they had done in the early days. But the wolf from Egypt was devoured by the wolf from Babylon, and Judah changed masters; Jehoiakim attempted to rebel against Nebuchadnezzar, the Assyrian king, with disastrous war as a result; his son Jehoiachin, who followed him, was taken captive by Nebuchadnezzar, and carried off to Babylon, with all his courtiers, men-at-arms, and treasure; so Judah fell. The victor made Jehoiachin's uncle, Zedekiah, king of Jerusalem, an ironically empty honour, which, however, Zedekiah might have held indefinitely if he had not seen fit to rebel.

This rebellion brought down the final catastrophe. Nebuchadnezzar, after a long siege, captured Jerusalem, took Zedekiah to Riblah, where he was subjected to a court-martial. After killing his sons in his presence—the last sight he saw on earth—they tore out his eyes, bound him with fetters of brass, and carried him to Babylon. Nebuzaradan, commander-in-chief of the Assyrian forces, destroyed the walls of Jerusalem, burned the temple of the Lord and all the houses, and carried away in captivity every able-bodied man, leaving only the scum of the city to eke out what substance they could from the desolated land.

After the death of King Nebuchadnezzar, and after poor old Jehoiachin had been in a dungeon in Babylon thirty-seven years, Evilmerodach, the new king, took him out of prison, treated him with such kindness and consideration that his throne in the city was placed before the thrones of the numerous other captive kings which decorated the town, gave him fine garments to wear, a generous pension, and made him a daily guest at the royal table all the days of his life.

What a romantic history! And how amazed Jehoiachin must have been at the change in his fortunes! Writers of romance, there is a subject made to your hand.

The life of a nation is like the life of an individual. The Hebrews had weakened themselves by sin and apostasy to such an extent that they were at the mercy of an attack which they could easily have thrown back in the days of their vigour. They and they alone were responsible for their ultimate disgrace and ruin.

Daniel holds his place among the four major prophets in Hebrew literature by reason of the extraordinary strength of his character and his thrilling adventures. His book is brief, but packed with exciting incident. It will forever be the joy and delight of children, and it is full of significance to thoughtful men and women.

When Jehoiakim was on the throne of Judah and Nebuchadnezzar captured the town, he brought the princes of the blood royal and the finest specimens of young Hebrew manhood into his own palace in Babylon, and gave command that those who combined bodily and mental gifts should be given the best of food and the best of teaching, so that they might become proficient in the art and learning of the Chaldeans and forget their nativity and their religion. It was a clever attempt to force, gently but effectively, Babylonian Kultur on the children of Judah.

Among these brilliant youths were four of especial comeliness and promise—Daniel and three others. Their Hebrew names were changed into Belteshazzar, Shadrach, Meshach, and Abednego. It is curious that in popular parlance Daniel has always kept his Jewish name, while the other three—originally Hananiah, Mishael, and Azariah—will forever be remembered by their foreign appellations. Possibly in English this may be because of the melodious rhythm of the three taken together; probably because the original chronicler preserved the name of the prophet, while after a struggle he seems to have adopted the Babylonian names for the others.

In the foreign court Daniel was as popular as Joseph in the court of Pharaoh, and in many striking ways seems to have resembled his Hebrew prototype; he was clever, wise, well-spoken, irresistibly charming in manner, and a psychoanalyst of such skill that he interpreted dreams without the least difficulty.

But he and his three friends were conscientious objectors, and if they had not been popular with the guards, they would not have lived to become famous. Daniel positively refused to eat the meat and drink the wine from the king's table, and begged the chief officer to let them live on vegetables and water. The twentieth century antipathy to flesh and alcohol was then unknown; and the officer demurred, saying that this meagre diet would destroy their strength and beauty, so that he would get into trouble. Daniel proposed the same test that Benjamin Franklin proposed to the beer-drinkers in the London printing-office, namely, to have a competition. The officer finally consented. Then at the end of ten days Daniel and his friends appeared more fit than any of the others. No more was said; and they ate vegetables and drank water in peace.

Thus Daniel holds a place in history as the first vegetarian; he was far ahead of his time, and ought to be especially honoured to-day by all the numerous theorisers in diet whose preaching fills our land. There are so many just now who are so much more interested in dieting than in religion that Daniel ought to be canonised. For to-day hundreds of thousands neglect their souls, while to themselves they put these burning and primarily important questions: What shall we eat? and what shall we drink?

It so happened that King Nebuchadnezzar had a dream so vivid that it tormented him; even after he woke up, and daylight flooded the place, he could not drive it from his mind. He finally sent for all his magicians, sorcerers, astrologers, fortune-tellers, mediums—indeed, all the fakirs and professional frauds that in all times and countries have made and are making a rich income off human gulls—and he gave them terrifying information. They were not only to interpret the dream, but tell him what the dream was; being a wise king, he may have suspected them, and have taken this occasion to get rid of them all. For he told them that if they succeeded in giving him the nature of the dream and of the interpretation, they should be magnificently rewarded; if they failed they should all be disemboweled and their houses turned into dunghills.

They protested; they declared that if he wished an interpretation he must first tell them the dream. "Just what I thought you would say," he declared in a royal rage; "all you want is to gain time, so you can make up some cock-and-bull story." He at once made a proclamation that every "wise man" in the kingdom should be slain.

This of course included Daniel; he spoke with the captain of the guard, and sent word to the king that the royal curiosity would be satisfied. In a night vision Daniel received the truth; he was so delighted that he composed an especial song of thanksgiving. He petitioned the king to spare the lives of the magicians, and as soon as he was brought into the presence he told Nebuchadnezzar that this affair had nothing to do with sorcerers or astrologers; that there was a God in heaven who revealed secrets to those who followed and worshipped Him. It was therefore not through Daniel's cleverness, but through God's mercy, that he was able to give both dream and vision.

Then he narrated the dream—a great image appeared, with gold head, silver breast, brass thighs, iron legs, with an alloy of clay in the feet. A stone made without hands smote and smashed the feet; the image was pulverised, and the stone became a mountain and filled the earth. The interpretation: the present kingdom of Nebuchadnezzar was the gold head, which would be succeeded by gradually inferior kingdoms, which should finally go to ruin through dissension (iron and clay); then would come the Kingdom of God on earth, which should rule all nations.

Nebuchadnezzar, who had never bowed his haughty head before, fell on his face and worshipped Daniel, and gave him the same position that Joseph had held in Egypt; he became prime minister. Immediately he found state offices for his three friends, Shadrach, Meshach, and Abednego. Daniel was a good politician.

Some time after this event, the king caused to be erected a statue of gold about a hundred feet in height. He then issued the following silly ukase: whenever certain instrumental music should be played by the royal court orchestra, every person must fall down and worship the golden image. And so, with a few exceptions, they did. I wonder what the music was like.

The exceptions were Shadrach, Meshach, and Abednego. They were independent; they did their own thinking; they did not follow the herd; they served not the gods of the nation, nor did they care one iota for public sentiment. For the glory of poor human nature, be it remembered that out of every hundred thousand people, there are usually three who think for themselves. They must be prepared to share the doom of Shadrach, Meshach, and Abednego; for public opinion, when aroused, is a consuming fire.

Now, although Daniel had saved from ignominious death a horde of soothsayers, he and his three friends were not popular; which fact ought to be easily understood by those who know anything of human nature. These four foreigners were exalted office-holders, high in royal favour, and therefore the object of sharp and malignant envy.

The three non-conformists were as prominent as torches on a dark night; when the music sounded and the population fell flat and grovelled, these three gentlemen apparently heard nothing and noticed nothing; they simply went on tranquilly with whatever undertaking they had in hand.

News of their defiance was brought to the king, who had a typically regal rage. He sent for them, and asked them if the report of their behaviour was correct; if so, they would be cast into the burning fiery furnace, and where was there any God who could deliver them? Their answer is magnificent in its courage and independence. "We are not careful to answer thee in this matter"—that is, we are not in the least worried. There is a God who can deliver us, even from the midst of the flames—but then comes the splendid conclusion, the finest thing they said: *even if He does not,* we positively refuse to serve thy gods or bow down to thine image. There spoke true men and true believers—though He slay me, yet will I trust in Him.

Nebuchadnezzar's face grew even hotter than his furnace; in a blazing fury he commanded that the furnace be seven times increased in temperature. Which shows what a fool he was; for if he had wished to make them suffer, he ought to have had a nice, slow fire. The result was that the athletic executioners who took hold of the three victims, to cast them into the furnace, got a little too near the door thereof; tongues of flame darted out and destroyed them all. Whereas, to the amazement of the king, who had attended the ceremony in person at a safe distance, Shadrach, Meshach, and Abednego lost nothing in the fire but their fetters; they walked up and down in the roaring flames and seemed to like the climate; furthermore, they were under the protection of some divinity, for Nebuchadnezzar thought he saw an angel walking with them.

Then Nebuchadnezzar came near to the mouth of the burning fiery furnace, and spake, and said, Shadrach, Meshach, and Abednego, ye servants of the most high God, come forth, and come hither. Then Shadrach, Meshach, and Abednego came forth of the midst of the fire. And the princes, governors, and captains, and the king's counsellors, being gathered together, saw these men, upon whose bodies the fire had no power, nor was an hair of their head singed, neither were their coats changed, nor the smell of fire had passed on them.

The king was enormously impressed. The salamandric three were promoted, and it was commanded that any man who said one word against the Hebrew religion should be cut in pieces.

Nebuchadnezzar had another dream, and he sent for the great psycho-analyst, after trying without success the wisdom of the magicians; observe that nothing can cure one from going to mediums, once one has got the habit. Their ignorance and fraud may be proved, but they can usually do a good business even with old customers. Daniel was "aston-ied for one hour" when he heard the dream, and the king, instead of being angry, told him not to worry if he could not interpret it. But Daniel was not silent because he did not know the right answer; he was silent because he *did* know it. He was forced to tell the great king that a time was coming when he should be driven from power, and live like an ox in the field until he was sufficiently humbled to recognise God. Then all these things would be added unto him again.

Exactly one year after this conversation, Nebuchadnezzar was walking in the palace grounds, swelling with conceit, when there fell a voice from heaven, and within an hour he was driven out in disgrace, and ate grass in the pasture like a beast of the field. And thus he continued doing for a long time.

Personally I have no doubt this regimen was as good for his body as for his pride. The royal digestion was undoubtedly upset by high living on meats, dainties, pastry, and wine; so that to eat for many months lettuce, and cress, and cereals, and to drink only water, was a necessary change. It brought him back to reason and health. In the happiness of humility he took up again the cares of state, and until his death worshipped the God of Truth and Righteousness, as do all kings who retain or regain their sanity.

Nebuchadnezzar never forgot the religion he had acquired through vegetation, but his son Belshazzar, who succeeded him on the throne, was frivolous and dissipated, overfond of feasting and strong liquors. One night he arranged a magnificent state banquet, one thousand sitting down to dinner in a vast hall. The king, flushed with wine, ordered the holy vessels of the temple of Jerusalem to be brought, and he, the princes and the ladies of the court, all drank out of them. In the midst of the revelry there appeared a Hand, writing on the wall, and the king was troubled. He could see the Hand but not the words. The same old mediums made the same old failure to pass the examination. The queen, who seems to have been sitting up, although not present at the feast, listened to the sudden silence in the banquet hall, more noticeable than cheers: she entered the room, and informed the king that his father, when in a quandary, invariably consulted a wise Hebrew named Daniel. Accordingly, Daniel was aroused and brought into the presence. He was informed that if he could properly interpret the mystic handwriting he should be clothed in scarlet, wear a chain of gold, and be the third ruler in the kingdom.

Daniel was harsh and rude in his reply to these gracious words; he told the king to keep his gifts or bestow them elsewhere; this remark he followed by a denunciation of Belshazzar's career, comparing him unfavourably with his deceased father. At that moment the Hand vanished and the words appeared. The writing on the wall, said Daniel—and we can feel the suspense in the great room—is

MENE, MENE, TEKEL, UPHARSIN,

which, being interpreted, is as follows: The first two words mean that God has numbered your kingdom, and reached the end of it; TEKEL means you are weighed, and are a featherweight; UPHARSIN or PERES signifies that your kingdom is divided, and the Medes and Persians will take it.

Instead of killing Daniel for his insolence, Belshazzar immediately gave orders and the prophet was clothed in scarlet, a chain of gold put round his neck, and he was proclaimed the third ruler in the kingdom. One cannot praise too highly the sportsmanship and honesty and magnanimity of the king. This command was the last he uttered, for that very night he was killed, and Darius the Mede mounted the throne.

The next adventure of Daniel is one of the world's favourite stories, and peculiarly appeals to the vivid imagination of children. It would be difficult to find anyone who had not heard of Daniel in the den of lions. His other exploits are sufficiently remarkable; but the lions immortalised him.

As Daniel had been a prominent statesman under both Nebuchadnezzar and Belshazzar, so Darius, who became king at the age of sixty-two, made Daniel prime minister, "because an excellent spirit was in him." The courtiers and politicians looked at him with green eyes and tried to find something wrong in his administration. But this was impossible, for he was both able and honest. Finally they remembered that he had never surrendered to the state-church, and in this fact saw an opportunity to ruin him. It seems that the laws of the Medes and the Persians were stiffer than the United States Constitution; once decreed they could be neither modified nor broken. Accordingly these plotters induced King Darius to establish a decree that for the next thirty days no person should ask a petition of either God or man, but only of the king. The penalty for disobedience was the den of lions. Now kings are just as easily flattered as other men; and Darius signed the decree complacently.

Daniel, who never lacked the courage of his convictions, went into his house, opened the windows toward Jerusalem, and there in sight of the passers in the street, knelt down and prayed three times a day to Jehovah. Word was immediately brought to Darius, who was terribly depressed; he not only loved Daniel personally, but knew his value as a statesman. He set in motion all the royal influence, and worked till sunset to find some method by which Daniel could be saved. Impossible. Just before Daniel was thrown into the lion-pit, the king whis- pered to him, "Thy God will save thee." A stone was rolled up to the den's mouth and sealed with the king's own seal.

Darius passed a much more restless night than Daniel; he ate no supper; he forbade the court orchestra to play the usual evening concert; he slept not a wink. At the first streak of dawn, he hastened to the den of lions and sobbed and wailed and called on the name of Daniel, asking if his God had saved him. Imagine the king's ecstasy when the familiar voice of the prime minister came cheerily out of the pit, saying: "Long live the King. My God hath sent his angel, and hath shut the lions' mouths, that they have not hurt me."

Then Daniel was taken up into safety, and the men who had accused him under the espionage act were cast into the den of lions, together with their wives and children, whose shrieks must have drowned the roar of the huge beasts. Now the lions, whose appetite had been sharpened to a razor edge by the night-long contemplation of Daniel, leaped upon this fresh supply of human meat and tore them all to pieces before the visitors had reached the bottom of the den.

Then Darius made a new decree to the effect that the religion of Daniel should be established as the state church, and that in every province the people should fear Jehovah; and Daniel continued high in favour both in the reign of Darius the Mede and in the reign of his successor, Cyrus the Persian.

The remainder of the book of Daniel is taken up with strange prophecies and stranger mathematics; in the attempt to solve these enigmas, the population of madhouses has been increased.

The lack of national bias so characteristic of the purely historical books of Samuel, of the Kings and the Chronicles, is by no means in evidence either in Daniel or in Esther; these two books, containing some of the best stories to be found anywhere in literature, are frankly written to glorify the Hebrew nation; they are warmly patriotic, the intention being to show that even during the captivity there were no men like the Hebrews, and no God like Jehovah. Even in the darkest hours they were a race of heroes and heroines. This bond of national pride unites the story of Daniel with the story of Esther; one great man and one great woman upheld the splendour of Israel in a strange land.

But there is this difference between them: the book of Daniel is deeply religious, and is an offering before Jehovah; the book of Esther is not religious at all, and is the only book in the Bible which does not mention the name of God. It is simply a superb drama, a drama so thrilling that it has been repeatedly transferred to the stage.

The mighty King Ahasuerus (Xerxes) gave a state dinner at Shushan (Susa), to inaugurate a world's fair which should last one hundred and eighty days, in which the riches and glory of his kingdom should be fittingly celebrated. When the exposition was over he gave a special feast to commemorate the occasion, a feast continuing for a week. This feasting was held in the palace garden at Susa, which had been decorated for the occasion in the most lavish style. There were pillars of marble, to which were attached curtains of gorgeous colours; the couches were of solid gold and silver, placed on a pavement of red, blue, black, and white marble. The king's special stock of wine was opened, and every guest was allowed to drink as much as he pleased. The result was what might have been expected.

Queen Vashti gave a special feast at the same time for the ladies of honour. I wish we knew more about her, for she must have been an interesting woman, with a mind of her own. Our forefathers, who tried to extract some piety out of every page in the Bible, believed she was stubborn, rebellious and wicked; the sin of pride was always reprehensible, but particularly so in women. The New England primer said

Vashti for pride
Was set aside.

As a matter of fact, I have nothing but commendation for her behaviour.

On the seventh day of this general debauch, the king was exceedingly drunk, and was bragging of the beauty of his queen. By a natural but regrettable impulse, he determined that she should be publicly exhibited before all the company, that they might see for themselves her shapely beauty. She was accordingly sent for; but having no desire to be paraded before the revellers, she flatly refused to come, showing more regard for her dignity and modesty than for the king's alcoholic caprices. Perhaps she believed that when he became sober again he would condemn her for such an exhibition and discard her forever. Anyhow, she refused. The king flew into that kind of rage that so frequently accompanies drunkenness, and wondered just what particular punishment might fit this crime.

There followed a conversation which, read in the light of the twentieth century, is decidedly amusing. The courtiers told the king that unless Vashti were deposed there would be no keeping the ladies down. Her obstinacy would be known everywhere, and wives would get the idea that they, too, might follow her example and set up their wills against their husbands, which simply would not do. What would become of society if women should feel independent, and not be subject to their lords and masters?

Accordingly, King Xerxes promulgated a law that throughout the kingdom every man should rule in his own house and the wives should give honour to their husbands, both great and small. This was not the last time that an attempt has been made to change human nature by legislation; it probably had the usual result. Can't you see in certain households capable wives sniffing contemptuously when their irresolute husbands quoted the law?

Then it was decided that the whole country should be searched for fair virgins, just as in the twentieth century a prize is given for the prettiest girl, and her picture is published in the papers, followed by an increase in her correspondence. All these village beauties were to be paraded before the king, so that he might pick a new queen.

Now it happened that in Susa there lived a certain Mordecai, who was a Hebrew of the tribe of Benjamin, and of the family of Kish, from which Saul, the first king of Israel, had sprung. As King Saul had come from the family of Kish in Benjamin, so Esther, the queen of Persia, came from the same family, and carried on the royal traditions. Although the children of Israel were in subjection, by clever manipulation they managed to get one of their own kingly stock on the conqueror's throne.

Esther was the daughter of Mordecai's uncle; I think that makes her his cousin, but I am not sure, not being strong on genealogy; her father and mother were dead, and she was penniless; but her face was her fortune, as we shall see. King Cophetua and the beggar maid—a favourite combination in romance.

Mordecai gave her some shrewd private coaching, and when her turn came to be shown to the king, he forgot all the other virgins and crowned her queen. Meanwhile, Mordecai, who sat in the king's gate, had discovered a conspiracy against the life of Xerxes; he informed Esther, who in her turn told her royal spouse; the plotters were seized and hanged on a tree, and the whole story set down in the state chronicles.

Prime Minister Haman was a pompous and conceited ass, who strutted conspicuously in public and enjoyed seeing the people bow down and do homage wherever he appeared; he loved to be saluted. Now just as Shadrach, Meshach, and Abednego had taken an independent attitude in the days of Nebuchadnezzar, Mordecai behaved in the same fashion in these times; when Haman passed the king's gate, Mordecai not only gave no salute, he did not take the trouble to rise from his chair. Like all little men dressed in authority, Haman could not endure this. When the courtiers remonstrated with Mordecai and asked him why he would not salute, he answered proudly, "I am a Jew." Haman therefore determined to destroy the entire Hebrew population.

These people were scattered abroad in every province, as they have been ever since; accordingly, with the king's consent, a decree was sent forth to north, south, east, and west that on a certain day they should be exterminated. Xerxes and Haman sat down to drink confusion to the Jews; but the city of Susa was perplexed.

Esther, carefully tutored by Mordecai, risked her life by appearing before the king unrequested; but she was looking uncommonly pretty that day and knew her power. The king told her in his enthusiasm that he would give her anything she asked for. She made the strange request that she would like a little dinner party of three—Xerxes, Haman, and herself. When Haman received his invitation, he expanded and did what many a man has done—bragged to his wife. Yet he added that he could not have unalloyed happiness so long as that stubborn Mordecai looked at him disdainfully. He suspected in his heart that Mordecai's cynical eyes appraised him at his true worth; his self-confidence was shaken, and he could not enjoy life so long as he had any doubt of his own greatness.

The sweets of popularity are sometimes embittered by one shrewd dissenter.

Zeresh could not really have loved such a preposterous fool as Haman, even though she was pleased with her social position; in her advice to her husband, she may have had some notions of her own. She suggested that he have erected a gallows so high that everybody in town could see its burden; then when the king is enjoying his dinner, to get his consent to decorate this lofty gibbet with Mordecai.

There followed a scene which seems strangely modern. On that night the king could not sleep, and after turning over, counting sheep, and trying to get his whirling mind out of the gear of care, he finally did what everyone has done; he decided to have light made, and to read awhile. Accordingly they brought before him what corresponded to the Congressional Record and began to read aloud, thinking the result would be certain; but when they reached the story of the conspiracy discovered by Mordecai, to their amazement the king sat up excitedly and asked if anything had been done for this man. Nothing.

It is at this point that the famous story has given the most delight to readers in all nations; for human nature enjoys nothing more than to see a rascal paid in his own coin, or, as Hamlet expressed it, to see the engineer hoist with his own petard. Hamlet's remark is particularly applicable in this case, for Haman was certainly hoisted.

The king sent for Haman, and asked him what ought to be done to the man whom the king delighteth to honour. Haman naturally took this remark to himself, and suggested a public parade. Imagine his feelings when he was told to hurry and escort Mordecai through the streets. After this long draught of wormwood, he went home to his wife in quite different spirits from those which haloed his departure. She calmly told him to expect the worst. While he was in this state of humiliation and fear, the chamberlains came to bring him to the banquet *à trois*.

In the midst of this little feast, Queen Esther suddenly rose and dramatically denounced him to the king, who rushed out into the garden to cool off. He returned and asked a question, in response to which a chamberlain informed him that the lofty gallows erected by Haman was convenient. Accordingly, Haman was hanged on the gibbet he had erected for his foe, and the king felt better.

The story ends with a patriotic flourish. Queen Esther followed up her success by getting the decree against the Jews reversed. The intended victims turned the tables and had the pleasure of slaughtering hundreds of their enemies. They "did what they would unto those that hated them." It was a field day. When the list of casualties was presented to Xerxes, he glanced over it with some interest and asked if there was anything else the queen desired. It appeared that she wished that the ten sons of Haman, who had already been slain, should also be publicly hanged; which was done.

Imagine the pride with which subsequent Hebrews of later times read the following three verses, a consolation for the conquest of their country:

And Mordecai went out from the presence of the king in royal apparel of blue and white, and with a great crown of gold, and with a garment of fine linen and purple: and the city of Shushan rejoiced and was glad. The Jews had light, and gladness, and joy, and honour. And in every province, and in every city, whithersoever the king's commandment and his decree came, the Jews had joy and gladness, a feast and a good day. And many of the people of the land became Jews; for the fear of the Jews fell upon them.

X

THE APOCRYPHA

A Somewhat Neglected but Interesting Section of the Bible—A Spirited Debate—What is the Strongest Thing in the World?—Daring of the Young Men— The Pessimism of Ignorance—Proper Attitude Toward Grief and Death—Dogs in the Bible—Judith and Holofernes—Patriotic Propaganda—Character of Judith—Comparison With Esther—A Discussion of Materialism—The Love of Beauty—Etiquette and Table Manners—Right Use of Wine—Apostrophe to Death—Susanna and the Elders—A Daniel Come to Judgment—Alexander the Great—Career of Judas Maccabeus—Fighting With Elephants—Wisdom, Valour, and Self-government of the Romans—An Ideal Editor—His Pleasant Humour—Torture of the Martyrs—The Mother and Her Seven Sons—The Editor's Farewell.

The books of the Apocrypha are among the most interesting parts of the Bible; they contain excellent stories, deep wisdom, keen wit, shrewd observation of life, with a continual revelation of human nature. They have been unduly neglected not only by the public, but by Bible students; but they will richly repay an attentive reading. As they are generally unknown to children, one comes to them in mature years with fresh eyes; one is unhampered by previous conceptions of their doctrinal or moral significance; it is almost as if a man of forty read the Psalms or *Hamlet* for the first time.

At the beginning of the Apocrypha, we come upon one of the noblest passages in the Bible; it is in the third and fourth chapters of the First Book of Esdras. It is in the form of a short story, and is an answer to this eternal question, What is the strongest thing in the world? The answer awarded the prize is precisely the one that would meet with the approval of the majority of thoughtful men and women in the twentieth century.

King Darius had given a great state feast, and while he was sleeping off the effects, three young gentlemen of his bodyguard wrote three sentences in competition and slipped them under his pillow. When he rose up, he called upon all the princes and the governors and the chiefs of the army and took his place on the throne in the royal hall of judgment; and in the presence of a vast concourse the three young men were summoned and requested to read and defend their opinions; the prize to be awarded by popular vote.

The first had written, *Wine is the strongest*. This statement he defended by showing how wine transformed the character and personality of those who indulged in it, how when they were drunk not only their behaviour but their whole point of view was different from their normal condition; and he insisted, with many amusing examples cited for corroboration, that an element which could so change the very heart of man must be the strongest thing in the world. It is interesting to remember that every one of the examples given by the speaker is just as noticeable to-day as then.

There is no equality in the world like that produced by drunkenness; no matter what their talents or social position, wealth or intellect or disposition may be in hours of soberness, drunken men are all on the same plane, both with their contemporaries and with those who have been in the grave three thousand years. One might say that alcohol puts all its victims on the same plane with a spirit level.

The second had written, *The king is strongest*. Then he proceeded to pay tribute to the supreme power of kings, giving many illustrations both in times of peace and in times of war; his eloquence did not conceal his irony, which was in fact so thinly veiled that it is surprising that Darius did not interrupt him with a reprimand. Man, said the speaker, is the highest form of strength produced on the planet, and as the king is always the chief and ruler of men, he must be the strongest thing in the world. Then he showed how both war and taxation depended on the caprice of the king; how the lives of his subjects were in the hollow of his hand; how some would go to war and others work on farms, merely at the king's pleasure; and then, with all the spoils that they had won by blood and sweat, they brought them humbly to the sole profiteer—the king. And while thousands of his subjects were thus fighting and working, "he lieth down, he eateth and drinketh, and taketh his rest." Surely the world affords no such example of strength as the king.

He made out a good case for his own time, and for many future generations; but not forever. He had on his side human statutes, but not natural law. The curious thing to a student of history is the long endurance of men and women under the caprices and cruelties of tyrants—why should they have enjoyed such arbitrary power for so many centuries? And, indeed, what the orator said was true of the Tsar Nikolas and the Kaiser Wilhelm so late as 1917; but it is true no longer. Our time (I hope) has put the last nail in the coffin of royalty. And it is worth remembering that Absolutism got its deathblow not from the wisdom, intelligence, and courage of the people, but solely through its own excesses and madness. Had the Tsar ruled with anything resembling wisdom and forbearance and consideration, he might have died in his bed; had

Wilhelm felt any limitations this side of divinity, he might to-day still be on the throne.

The third had written, *Women are strongest: but above all things Truth beareth away the victory.*

This man Zorobabel—the only one whose name is given—was an orator, an observer and a philosopher ; he spoke not only for his age, but for all time. He gave many piquant examples of the terrific power of women, in which he is supported not only by Hebrew history, but by the novelists and dramatists of the twentieth century. It was evident that he believed he could speak freely; for he did not hesitate to show the superiority of women to the king himself; and he pointed out something that has been the theme of many an American novel: that men are really the slaves of women.

Yea, and if men have gathered together gold and silver, or any other goodly thing, do they not love a woman which is comely in favour and beauty? And letting all those things go, do they not gape, and even with open mouth fix their eyes fast on her; and have not all men more desire unto her than unto silver or gold, or any goodly thing whatsoever?...

By this also ye must know that women have dominion over you: do ye not labour and toil, and give and bring all to the woman?...
Yea, many there be that have run out of their wits for women, and become servants for their sakes.
Many also have perished, have erred, and sinned, for women.
And now do ye not believe me? is not the king great in his power? do not all regions fear to touch him?
Yet did I see him and Apame the king's concubine, the daughter of the admirable Bartacus, sitting at the right hand of the king,
And taking the crown from the king's head, and setting it upon her own head; she also struck the king with her left hand.
And yet for all this the king gaped and gazed upon her with open mouth: if she laughed upon him, he laughed also: but if she took any displeasure at him, the king was fain to flatter, that she might be reconciled to him again.
O ye men, how can it be but women should be strong, seeing they do thus?
Then the king and the princes looked one upon another: so he began to speak of the truth.

After paying an eloquent tribute to the permanence and indestructibility of truth, he burst out passionately:

Wine is wicked, the king is wicked, women are wicked, all the children of men are wicked, and such are all their wicked works; and there is no truth in them; in their unrighteousness also they shall perish.

As for the truth, it endureth, and is always strong; it liveth and conquereth for evermore.

Then all the people shouted with enthusiasm:

Great is Truth, and mighty above all things.

Here is a verdict ratified to-day by Science, Art, and Religion.

In the fourth chapter of the Second Book of Esdras we find a number of searching questions, questions that have tormented the mind of man since Adam began to think. In a few picturesque words, we are given precisely the same conclusions arrived at in 1781 by Immanuel Kant—that the human mind cannot *know* the things beyond its reach, although those are the things it most ardently desires to understand. The angel Uriel tells the enquirer Esdras that if he cannot give the exact weight of the fire, or the precise measurement of the blast of the wind, or call again the day that is past, he must not expect to be able to grasp the Infinite Mind. And Uriel, after putting some more questions, declared:

For like as the ground is given unto the wood, and the sea to his floods: even so they that dwell upon the earth may understand nothing but that which is upon the earth: and he that dwelleth above the heavens may only understand the things that are above the height of the heavens.

Esdras had expressed a sentiment that has driven many in later times to madness and to suicide.

It were better that we were not at all, than that we should live still in wickedness, and to suffer, and not to know wherefore.

But Uriel gave as we see limitations to human knowledge, in which he is supported by many modern writers. If I understand at all that extraordinary play, *Beyond Human Power,* by Björnson, it was written to show the danger and folly of attempting to grasp things forever beyond the reach of the human intellect. Yet the desire to do so is inherent in man, and its negation is a cause of pessimism. As Esdras puts it, "We pass away out of the world as grasshoppers, and our life is astonishment and fear."

The sorrow and desolation caused by the years 1914-1918, the general and the particular grief, one will find analysed and discussed in the tenth chapter of the Second Book of Esdras. A woman had lost her son, had refused the consolation offered by her neighbours, had refused both meat and drink, had refused to take up the burden of life again, and had insisted that she would spend the remaining moments of her time on earth in wailing and lamentation, living only in the memory of her son. For this she is sharply rebuked by Esdras, who told her that in the universal distress of the whole nation, the entire country being in mourning, she must not indulge in selfish sorrow. There was work to be done, and she must live out her own life, and not throw it away.

For ask the earth, and she shall tell thee, that it is she which ought to mourn for the fall of so many that grow upon her.
For out of her came all the first, and out of her shall all others come, and behold, they walk almost all into destruction, and a multitude of them is utterly rooted out.
Who then should make more mourning than she, that hath lost so great a multitude; and not thou, which art sorry for one.

The healing effects of Nature have never been more wisely set forth; in spite of appalling losses and unspeakable disasters, nature goes quietly on with her eternal work of reparation and of new growth.

Now therefore keep thy sorrow to thyself, and bear with a good courage that which hath befallen thee.
For if thou shalt acknowledge the determination of God to be just, thou shalt both receive thy son in time, and shalt be commended among women.

While it would be both futile and flippant to attempt to minimise the grief of a parent who lost a son in the war, I believe that no one has a right to live in a tomb. No one should live only in the memory of those who are gone; let the vanished figure be an influence rather than an annihilator; let it lift up, rather than crush. For not only is the gift of life too precious to be thrown away, there is always work to be done. The tender-hearted Teacher was neither indifferent nor cruel when He said, "Let the dead bury their dead, and come and follow me."

It is rather curious that in the Bible so little mention is made of family pets. Considering the exalted place of the Dog in literature, and how in Sanskrit tales and in Homer he was so beloved and respected, why is it that the Hebrews ignored him? Both in the Old and New Testament the word dog is a term of reproach, and although there certainly were family dogs in Palestine—they ate of the crumbs that fell from the master's table, and licked the sores of Lazarus the beggar—they are never spoken of affectionately, nor do they play any part in the daily life of man. For this reason, the sole reference that I can remember of a companionable dog, found in the eleventh chapter of Tobit, is worth recording:

So they went their way, and the dog went after them.

The book of Tobit also contains much sound advice, especially in Chapters IV and XII.

It is good to keep close the secret of a king, but it is honourable to reveal the works of God. Do that which is good, and no evil shall touch you.

In dramatic intensity, the story of Judith rivals that of Esther. The Assyrian king sent out General Holofernes, with an enormous army, which conquered and laid waste many cities and farms; when the victorious host reached Syria, the inhabitants were in mortal terror. Most of the coast towns threw open their gates, paid tribute, and received him with song and dance.

But in Jerusalem, where the children of Judah had only lately returned from captivity, it was decided to resist the invader; they fortified the mountains round about, and prepared to withstand a siege. Holofernes heard of their determination, and he asked Captain Achior, the Ammonite, who these people were, and why they did not surrender like the people of the west. Achior gave him briefly the whole history of the children of Israel from the days of Moses to the present date. Achior said their strength and their weakness depended entirely on whether they were or were not true to their God; and he advised finding out, for if they are now true to Jehovah, said he, you can do nothing with them. Their God will fight for them.

Honest Achior was severely rebuked for his warning, and Holofernes insolently said that he would make the mountains drunk with Jewish blood and choke their fields with dead bodies. General Holofernes then treated Achior exactly as Abraham Lincoln treated Vallandingham; he sent him into the enemy's camp, where the Jews received him gladly, comforted him, and listened with intense interest to his report of the advancing host.

Holofernes drew near to the city of Bethulia, and cut off the water supply, which came from without the walls; so that the inhabitants were soon suffering from both hunger and thirst.

Judith was a beautiful widow, whose husband had died from sunstroke. For three years she had remained absolutely faithful to his memory, and although by reason of her beauty and wealth she was much sought after, she seemed indifferent to all men. "And there was none that gave her an ill word; for she feared God greatly."

The people told Ozias, the mayor of the town, that he must surrender to Holofernes; he pleaded for five days more. Judith sent for the chiefs in the city government, and told them to trust in the Lord, reminding them of His favours to Abraham, Isaac, and Jacob. She then said that she and her maid were going out of the city gate that night, and that Ozias must not reveal the fact nor make any enquiry.

Then Judith, after a long prayer, took off her widow's weeds, washed her body all over with water, anointed herself with perfume, arranged her hair in the most attractive style, and put on her "garments of gladness;" this last phrase being perhaps the origin of the familiar term in American slang. She "decked herself bravely, to allure the eyes of men," and, accompanied by her maid, she went straight to the Assyrian camp. The soldiers were instantly captivated by her beauty and grace of manner, and she informed them that she must see Holofernes as she had a plan by which he could capture the town from which she had just escaped. So like a future Monna Vanna, she went into the tent of the alien.

As she went, the soldiers said to one another, "Who would despise this people, that have among them such women?" And their desire for conquest was considerably sharpened by the sight of her.

General Holofernes came forth from his tent in all his glory, with silver lamps going before him. Judith had not the slightest difficulty in twisting the great man around her little finger, for her beauty shone out in the lamplight, and her words of deceit and flattery possessed him immediately. He said fatuously, "And now thou art both beautiful in thy countenance, and witty in thy words." For three days she kept him at arm's length, with the thrust and parry of skilful language, but finally she consented to dine with him in his tent.

And Holofernes took great delight in her, and drank much more wine than he had drunk at any time in one day since he was born.

All the guards and attendants were sent away, the tent was closed, and Judith was left alone with Holofernes, who had fallen into a drunken sleep. She came to his couch, drew his sword, prayed for strength, and with her left hand seized the hair of his head, and with her right hand smote him in the neck twice with all her might, so that his head was severed from his body. Carrying the head in a bag, she and her maid hastened to the city of Bethulia.

When she was still afar off, Judith gave a loud, triumphant call to the watchman at the gate, so loud that many in the city were awakened, and rushed to the walls. There they made a huge bonfire for a light, and in the midst of the glare Judith dramatically held aloft the head of Holofernes. It was a great scene, never to be forgotten in the annals of the town.

It is significant of the immense respect that the citizens held for her that every word of her story was accepted without qualification. There were no doubters, like the husband of Monna Vanna. Judith had taken the head of Holofernes without paying anything for it—except the crucifixion of her nerves.

Then all the women of Israel ran together to see her, and blessed her, and made a dance among them for her: and she took branches in her hand, and gave also to the women that were with her.

And they put a garland of olive upon her and her maid that was with her, and she went before all the people in the dance, leading all the women: and all the men of Israel followed in their armour with garlands, and with songs in their mouths.

Judith received frequent offers of marriage and refused them all, remaining constant to the memory of her husband, who must have been an extraordinary character to leave so ineffaceable an impression. Perhaps Judith also thought that her visit to the Assyrian camp might disturb the thoughts of a new husband, even though her absolute innocence was universally accepted. One can never predict the subtle reaches of the poison of a jealous imagination. Perhaps she had seen enough of men. As it was, she was free and independent, the First Lady of the town. It is pleasant to observe that she made her servant a free woman, because of her courage and fidelity in accompanying her mistress to the enemy's lines. Judith lived to be a hundred and five years old, and was buried beside her husband.

She is one of the national heroines. As Esther saved her people by winning the favour of their Persian ruler, so Judith saved them by beheading their enemy. It is worth remembering that although they were both clever and accomplished women, they won their triumphs by their personal beauty, and by their confidence in it. Of Judith, the account says, "Her beauty took his mind prisoner." And the all-but-miraculous ability of women to look one emotion and feel another, something forever beyond the reach of men, is well expressed in the apocryphal addition to the book of Esther:

And she was ruddy through the perfection of her beauty, and her countenance was cheerful and very amiable: but her heart was in anguish for fear.

Her terror was kept down, for she actually controlled the flow of her blood by the power of her will; just as the great actress Duse could blush whenever she wished.

The book of Judith resembles the book of Esther again in being patriotic propaganda, and was doubtless taught to the Hebrew children in the schools.

Painters and dramatists have made free use of Judith and Holofernes; the latest play on this theme is by Arnold Bennett, who has managed the dialogue with his accustomed skill and vivacity.

In the Book of the Wisdom of Solomon, which contains many passages of striking and unexpected beauty, there is, in the thirteenth chapter, a remarkable discussion of the materialists, in which they are praised for their love of beauty and strength, and condemned because they do not penetrate through the wonders of nature to the Divine Artist. This passage is surely as applicable in the twentieth century as when first written.

Surely vain are all men by nature, who are ignorant of God, and could not out of the good things that are seen know him that is: neither by considering the works did they acknowledge the workmaster; But deemed either fire, or wind, or the swift air, or the circle of the stars, or the violent water, or the lights of heaven, to be the gods which govern the world.

With whose beauty if they being delighted took them to be gods; let them know how much better the Lord of them is: for the first author of beauty hath created them.

But if they were astonished at their power and virtue, let them understand by them, how much mightier is he that made them. For by the greatness and beauty of the creatures proportion-ably the maker of them is seen. But yet for this they are the less to be blamed: for they per-adventure err, seeking God, and desirous to find him. For being conversant in his works they search him diligently, and believe their sight: because the things are beautiful that are seen. Howbeit neither are they to be pardoned. For if they were able to know so much, that they could aim at the world; how did they not sooner find out the Lord thereof?

The Book of Ecclesiasticus was written by a man of the world, and is filled not only with wisdom, but with a dry humour. Evidently opera and concert singers were then vain and difficult, and it was better to have a row of footlights always between them and the average man, for they seldom improved on acquaintance. The queen of song off the stage was often a conceited and petulant child. This has, of course, all been changed in our time. But in the ninth chapter, we are told:

Use not much the company of a woman that is a singer, lest thou be taken with her attempts.

Longevity was about the same then as now; for in Chapter XVIII, we read, "The number of a man's days at the most are an hundred years."

Those who talk all the time are justly regarded as among the most pestilential curses of the world; they were no more popular then than now, for in Chapter XXV it is said, "As the climbing up a sandy way is to the feet of the aged, so is a wife full of words to a quiet man."

The author of this book knew well that etiquette Was the next thing to godliness; there is no doubt that bad table manners have wrecked many homes, quenched the fire of love, and destroyed the good influence of many pious folks. In Chapter XXXI we receive a lesson in behaviour at meals, in which greediness and the famous "boarding-house reach" are both condemned. No woman should marry a man until she has seen him eating.

If thou sit at a bountiful table, be not greedy upon it, and say not, There is much meat on it...

Stretch not thine hand whithersoever it looketh, and thrust it not with him into the dish...

Eat, as it becometh a man, those things which are set before thee; and devour not, lest thou be hated.

Leave off first for manners' sake; and be not unsatiable, lest thou offend. When thou sittest among many, reach not thine hand out first of all.

Apparently there were times when politeness forced a gentleman to eat at his host's table, either when he was not hungry, or when the particular food was unpalatable. In the following verse a ready and easy way to preserve both one's manners and one's health is given:

And if thou hast been forced to eat, go forth, vomit, and thou shalt have rest.

An excellent method with parsnips.

It is unfortunate that the following advice given in this same chapter has not been followed by the world; if it had been heeded, we should not have been obliged to adopt in America a certain Constitutional Amendment.

Wine is as good as life to a man, if it be drunk moderately; what life is then to a man without wine? for it was made to make men glad.

Wine measurably drunk and in season bringeth gladness of the heart, and cheerfulness of the mind:

But wine drunken with excess maketh bitterness of the mind, with brawling and quarrelling.

The author was a "forward-looking man," for in this verse in the thirty-third chapter he seems to have foreseen a domestic problem in our time:

If thou have a servant, entreat him as a brother: for thou hast need of him, as of thine own soul: if thou entreat him evil, and he run from thee, which way wilt thou go to seek him?

Considering the towering position in modern life and in modern fiction held by the physician, the opening words of Chapter XXXVIII are significant:

Honour a physician with the honour due unto him for the uses which ye may have of him: for the Lord hath created him. . . . The skill of the physician shall lift up his head: and in the sight of great men he shall be in admiration.

All hero-worshippers, of whom I am one, will receive encouragement and stimulation from the magnificent passage in Chapter XLIV, beginning, "Let us now praise famous men." In these glorious verses homage is paid to statesmen, prophets, teachers, poets, musicians, philanthropists: "all these were honoured in their generations, and were the glory of their times." Then follows an eloquent tribute to all the unknown humble men and women who have in their days on earth done deeds of kindness and mercy.

Occasionally, in the midst of passages of shrewd wisdom, there comes in the style a sudden noble elevation:

O Death, how bitter is the remembrance of thee to a man that liveth at rest in his possessions, unto the man that hath nothing to vex him, and that hath prosperity in all things: yea, unto him that is yet able to receive meat! O Death, acceptable is thy sentence unto the needy, and unto him whose strength faileth, that is now in the last age, and is vexed with all things, and to him that despaireth, and hath lost patience!

Perhaps no part of the Apocrypha has had more influence on the art of painting than the story of Susanna, which has a book to itself. In European galleries, one becomes weary of the eternal repetition of the two old bearded peepers—Susanna and the elders are much better known on canvas than they are in the original narrative, which has also produced a proverb universally quoted whose source is all but unknown. The story brings out clearly the perverted folly of these aged judges, for there is no fool like an old fool. When they attempted to convict Susanna in the court, a young man named Daniel appeared, who is rather absurdly called "a young youth," but whose method of ascertaining truth was the reverse of absurd. He turned the tables, saved the virtuous lady, and destroyed the elders.

I suppose that very few when they read or quote from *The Merchant of Venice*, "A Daniel come to judgment!" realise that it is not from the book of Daniel, but from the book of Susanna, that Shakespeare obtained his example.

To those who are accustomed to make a distinction between sacred and profane history, the First Book of The Maccabees will produce something akin to a shock; for it opens with an account of Alexander the Great.

And it happened, after that Alexander, son of Philip, the Macedonian, who came out of the land of Chettiim, had smitten Darius, king of the Persians and Medes, that he reigned in his stead, the first over Greece.

And made many wars, and won many strongholds, and slew the kings of the earth.

And went through to the ends of the earth, and took spoils of many nations, insomuch that the earth was quiet before him; whereupon he was exalted, and his heart was lifted up.

And he gathered a mighty strong host, and ruled over countries, and nations, and kings, who became tributaries unto him. And after these things he fell sick, and perceived that he should die.

The history of many years is then summarised in a sentence, until we come to the villain of the book, Antiochus IV, surnamed Epiphanes, king of Syria. He endeavoured to put in place of Hebrew customs, worship and ritual, the Greek ideas and methods; he was resisted by the Jews, who found a great patriotic leader in Judas Maccabeus. The wars between Judas and the king took place in the second century before Christ, and are the subject of the First Book of the Maccabees. The narrative is exceedingly valuable as history, and of course is written from the patriotic point of view. Judas Maccabeus was one of five sons of Mattathias, a sturdy orthodox Jew, who stoutly resisted the victorious king, and called upon the fainthearted Hebrews to remember all that Jehovah had done for them since the time of Abraham. It is interesting there as everywhere to see how powerful a force is national tradition—how every heroic man and every heroic deed stands up out of the long past, as a living force.

When Mattathias came to die, he gathered his sons around him, and told them of the might of faith.

Fear not then the words of a sinful man: for his glory shall be dung and worms.

Today he shall be lifted up, but tomorrow he shall not be found, because he is returned into his dust, and his thought is come to nothing.

Wherefore, ye my sons, be valiant, and shew yourselves men in the behalf of the law; for by it shall ye obtain glory. . .

As for Judas Maccabeus, he hath been mighty and strong, even from his youth up: let him be your captain, and fight the battle of the people.

The accounts of the numerous battles that follow are spirited and dramatic; and the speeches of Judas are as fine as his deeds. After the death of Antiochus, his son came up and besieged Jerusalem, with a hundred thousand infantry, twenty thousand cavalry, and thirty-two trained elephants. The way these huge beasts were used in battle is interesting; they were shown the blood of grapes and mulberries to excite their fighting spirit.

And upon the beasts were there strong towers of wood, which covered every one of them, and were girt fast unto them with devices: there were also upon every one two and thirty strong men, that fought upon them, beside the Indian that ruled him.

In the eighth chapter of the First Book there is an interesting reference to the character and prestige of the Romans.

Now Judas had heard of the fame of the Romans, that they were mighty and valiant men, and such as would lovingly accept all that joined themselves unto them, and make a league of amity with them; And that they were men of great valour.

Then follows a recital of the conquest of the earth by the Romans, how they had subdued mighty kings, and all nations that resisted them, so that they really were the men of destiny.

Yet for all this none of them wore a crown, or was clothed in purple, to be magnified thereby:

Moreover how they had made for themselves a senate house, wherein three hundred and twenty men sat in council daily, consulting always for the people, to the end they might be well ordered:

And that they committed their government to one man every year, who ruled over all their country, and that all were obedient to that one, and that there was neither envy nor emulation among them.

Therefore a treaty was made between the Romans and the Jews. By these few verses which describe the Romans as they were appraised by aliens, we see how the genius of that people for both war and government was widely understood; and how it accounted for the power of Rome; it is by strikingly similar methods that the British Empire is the mightiest force in the world today. The Romans appealed to Judas Maccabeus as an eminently reasonable nation, men with whom a sensible man could talk and do business.

In the second chapter of the Second Book of the Maccabees there is a highly diverting passage, which ought to be read and deeply pondered by every person who writes a book or tells a story. Nearly all books, narratives, articles, sermons, and speeches are too long; nearly all could have been improved if their makers had practiced the divine art of omission and selection; if they had had an instinctive sense of what is important and what is superfluous; if they had known the value of emphasis; if they had felt any mercy.

It appears that the writer had before him a long history in five books, and he wisely and mercifully conceived it to be his duty to condense these five books into one. He well knew the task was one not lightly to be undertaken; that it would cost him immense labour and anxiety; but he had compassion on his readers, and determined to undertake the beneficent work of abridgment. This is the delightful way in which he writes his explanatory preface, so delightful a way that our hearts warm toward him, for we have all suffered greatly from long-winded orators and voluminous penmen.

All these things, I say, being declared by Jason of Cyrene in five books, we will assay to abridge in one volume.

For considering the infinite number, and the difficulty which they find that desire to look into the narrations of the story, for the variety of the matter;

We have been careful, that they that will read may have delight, and that they that are desirous to commit to memory might have ease, and that all into whose hands it comes might have profit.

Therefore to us, that have taken upon us this painful labour of abridging, it was not easy, but a matter of sweat and watching;

Even as it is no ease unto him that prepareth a banquet, and seeketh the benefit of others: yet for the pleasuring of many we will undertake gladly this great pains;

Leaving to the author the exact handling of every particular, and labouring to follow the rules of an abridgment . . .

Here then will we begin the story: only adding thus much to that which hath been said, that it is a foolish thing to make a long prologue, and to be short in the story itself.

It is curious that in those days we should find an editor of such admirable judgment and temper, and with that fine flavour of humour. He is a model.

The style of the abridgment is spirited and strong, carrying the reader irresistibly. There are pungent phrases here and there, as "one Auranus being the leader, a man far gone in years, and no less in folly."

In the description of the Hebrew martyrs, in Chapters VI and VII, the story is dramatic in the extreme, and must have stirred the blood and courage of the Jews for many generations. It seems that a victorious king endeavoured to make the captives eat swine's flesh, strictly forbidden by the Mosaic Law. He promised them every favour and kindness if they would submit, and the most horrible tortures if they refused. Once more, as in other cases in history, we see how the individual will is stronger not only than the fear of death, but stronger than the fear of frightful bodily and mental anguish. The tormentors took Eleazar, an old scribe, and forcibly fed him with pork; but he spit it forth, and gladly embraced torture. Then the executioners, being fond of the splendid old man, suggested that he could pretend to eat it, while really eating pure food secretly provided; but, to the glory not only of his nation, but of humanity, he replied:

For it becometh not our age, said he, in any wise to dissemble, whereby many young persons might think that Eleazar, being fourscore years and ten, were now gone to a strange religion,

And so they through mine hypocrisy, and desire to live a little time and a moment longer, should be deceived by me, and I get a stain to mine old age, and make it abominable.

He therefore went to the torture with a firm step and a cheerful face.

Then the king took seven brothers and their mother together. Each young man in turn was tortured so horribly that it makes the flesh of the reader creep, for it is impossible to read of such hellish devices without actual physical suffering. They were every one given the chance to recant; but they declined, and were slowly burned and flayed and hacked to pieces with their mother looking on.

But the mother was marvellous above all, and worthy of honourable memory: for when she saw her seven sons slain within the space of one day, she bare it with a good courage, because of the hope that she had in the Lord.

Yea, she exhorted every one of them in her own language, filled with courageous spirits; and stirring up her womanish thoughts with a manly stomach.

When there was only one left, the youngest son, the king asked the mother to urge him to conform so that his life might be spared:

And when he had exhorted her with many words, she promised him that she would counsel her son.

But she, bowing herself toward him, laughing the cruel tyrant in the face, spake in her country language on this manner: O my son, have pity upon me that bare thee nine months in my womb, and gave thee suck three years, and nourished thee, and brought thee up unto this age, and endured the troubles of education.

Then she counselled him to stand fast, and be worthy of his dead brothers, whose mangled corpses were before them. He then defied the king, and had the worst death of all; he was quickly followed by his mother.

At the end of the book, the abridging historian concludes quaintly:

And if I have done well, and as is fitting the story, it is that which I desired: but if slenderly and meanly, it is that which I could attain unto. For as it is hurtful to drink wine or water alone; and as wine mingled with water is pleasant, and delighteth the taste: even so speech finely framed delighteth the ears of them that read the story. And here shall be an end.

Whether drinking water alone was then hurtful or not, it is true that monotony in everything, whether in food, drink, or rhetoric, becomes dull; and in this author we have an early example of a thoroughly self-conscious literary artist, who practiced composition with pain and pleasure; the pain of strenuous effort, and the pleasure of devotion to his work.

XI

WISDOM AND PHILOSOPHY

Contemporary Value of the Book of Proverbs—The Same Channel—Is Experience Really the Best Teacher?—Human Wisdom—The Practical Guide-Book with a Touch of Poetry—Philosophy of Moderation—Quotable Value—Various Sins and Remedies— Disarmament—Diplomatic Value of Silence—Personal Honour—Shrewish Women—Inopportune Friends—Wisdom of Distrusting Oneself—Ulysses and the Sirens—St. Paul's Quotation—The Wonderful Words of Agur—Poetry and Mystery—The Ideal Woman—The Book of Ecclesiastes—Koheleth—Professor Jastrow—Philosophy of Pessimism—Chekhov's Monologue—John Galsworthy—The Preacher and the Scribe—Modernity of this Book—Compared with Omar Khayyam—Vanity of Vanities—Fallacy of Pessimism—The Splendid Poetry—The Last Chapter—Sorrows of Old Age—-The Admonition of the Scribe.

Whatever may be thought of the scientific value of the cosmogony of Genesis, however people may disagree as to the historicity of the deeds of Elisha, no matter how sceptical may be the general attitude toward the story of Jonah—the Book of Proverbs is not obsolete. It was written a long while ago, but is more contemporary than this morning's newspaper. It cannot become demoded; it has been, is, and always will be true; for it is founded on the eternal base of human nature; less subject to change than the solid rocks.

Mark Twain used to say that the Mississippi River had the habit of changing its channel overnight; so that on each trip the pilot must be alert. But the channel of human conduct has never altered; the chart therefore remains the same. In a world where we know so little, it is interesting to remember that for the main lines of action and behaviour our knowledge is sufficient. Wisdom and folly are now what they always have been. It is not necessary to be a fool in order to discover the results of folly. There are thousands of fools today sufficiently obliging to act as examples, lending freely their experience to the profit of observers.

It is often said that Experience is the best teacher; but this is true only when we gain by the experience of others. In the case of the sufferer, Experience is not the best teacher; because she charges more for her instruction than it is worth. It does you no good to learn how you ought to have conducted your business when you are bankrupt; it does not help you to learn the proper diet when you are dying from poison.

But ye have set at nought all my counsel, and would none of my reproof: I also will laugh at your calamity; I will mock when your fear cometh; When your fear cometh as desolation, and your destruction cometh as a whirlwind; when distress and anguish cometh upon you.

The Book of Proverbs is a collection of wise sayings founded on observation of life. It is a clear revelation of human nature, showing that in Hebrew history they had the same varieties of humanity that now walk the streets of Manhattan. It is often called Hebrew Wisdom, but it should be called Human Wisdom. It is a mingling of shrewdness and piety; energy and reverence. It does not point out every danger, but it shows the safe path. Its wisdom reaches far into the future; for though it does not tell us what is wrong with our automobile— such engines then being unknown—it tells us how to drive in security.

This famous Guide-Book is mainly given up to definite, practical instructions; but it also contains a splendid Hymn to Wisdom, wherein Wisdom is represented as being the first creation of God, practically coming into existence with the energy of the Divine Mind. Wisdom is older than the hills and the sea—and if mind be older than matter, it assuredly is. The prose of the book is specific, and meant to help travellers in this world in all emergencies, both private and public difficulties. The necessity of having a good education, relations of parents and children, wives and husbands, street-neighbours, value of hard work and the danger of shiftlessness, dangers of poverty and of wealth, civic duties both in the courts and in trade, restraint in food, drink, and speech, control of the sensual and angry passions, and how in general to conduct oneself in society.

I neither know nor care who wrote out all these proverbs; they are the accumulated wisdom and knowledge of many generations, brief and convenient summaries of conduct. The important thing is not, Who wrote them? or when were they written? but are they true? and if so, what use shall we make of them?

In the main, they teach the philosophy of moderation—perhaps never more needed than now, when so many are extremists.

The two wisest men of modern times are Goethe and Franklin; they were fond of writing aphorisms and epigrams, composing guides to life. All the wisdom of the great German and the great American may be rightly regarded as footnotes to the Book of Proverbs.

When a man thinks, talks, and acts well, he has behind him the support of centuries of experience; when he behaves badly, he is running counter to a force that has gained irresistible momentum by Time.

The percentage of alloy in this great Book is small, for nearly every verse is the pure metal, that which remains after having passed the sharpest and most searching tests. This is why they are so frequently quoted, and why without additional comment, they so often make a final answer to a proposition. It is well for public speakers and debaters to know this book; it is a quiver full of pointed arrows.

It is interesting to observe that in the Proverbs a specific application often follows a general suggestion; as if to say, Here is the general truth, and here a definite illustration.

Withhold not good from them to whom it is due, when it is in the power of thine hand to do it.

Say not unto thy neighbour: Go, and come again, and tomorrow I will give; when thou hast it by thee.

The author of the sixth chapter did not disdain to learn wisdom from the smallest animals; in his attack on laziness—a universal sin—he saw that a bug might have more brains than a man, and was therefore fitted to teach humanity.

Go to the ant, thou sluggard; consider her ways, and be wise:

Which having no guide, overseer, or ruler,

Provideth her meat in the summer, and gathereth her food in the harvest. How long wilt thou sleep, O sluggard? when wilt thou arise out of thy sleep? Yet a little sleep, a little slumber, a little folding of the hands to sleep: So shall thy poverty come as one that travelleth, and thy want as an armed man.

Much is said in these proverbs about strange women, who were then as now a menace to the individual and to society; there is one verse in the sixth chapter that sums up the whole question in a few words.

But whoso commiteth adultery with a woman lacketh understanding: he that doeth it destroyed! his own soul.

And dealing with this same vice, the wise man attempts to destroy the illusion by coupling consequences with conduct, in a dramatic sequence:

Stolen waters are sweet, and bread eaten in secret is pleasant.
But he knoweth not that the dead are there; and that her guests are in the depths of hell.

Apart from the exhortations to good behaviour, there are many passages which have nothing to do with ethics, but are simply revelations of the mind of man, shedding light in dark places, as:

Hope deferred maketh the heart sick.

The heart knoweth his own bitterness; and a stranger doth not intermeddle with his joy. Even in laughter the heart is sorrowful; and the end of that mirth is heaviness.

In the twentieth century we hear much talk of disarmament, both because of its expense, carrying burdensome taxation, and because nations know that they are not themselves to be trusted with many battleships, any more than a child can be trusted with toy pistols. But the sure way to disarm one's personal enemy is given in Chapter XV:

A soft answer turneth away wrath; but grievous words stir up anger.

Curious that nine out of ten persons still do all they possibly can to strengthen the malignant purpose and fighting power of their antagonists.

The limitless range of disaster brought about by fools is picturesquely set forth in this comparison: followed later by parental grief.

Let a bear robbed of her whelps meet a man, rather than a fool in his folly . . . the father of a fool hath no joy.

The strength of true friendship is interpreted in this verse:

A friend loveth at all times, and a brother is born for adversity.

The ease with which a reputation for wisdom can be gained and maintained, was understood perfectly, then as now:

Even a fool, when he holdeth his peace, is counted wise: and he that shutteth his lips is esteemed a man of understanding.

The reason for this is simple enough. It is the belief, usually well founded, that a fool cannot keep his mouth shut.

The apostle James, in his famous chapter on the untameable tongue, was perhaps thinking of the following verse:

Death and life are in the power of the tongue: and they that love it shall eat the fruit thereof.

The following passage undoubtedly was the cause of much lamentation among the children of Puritans:

Chasten thy son while there is hope, and let not thy soul spare for his crying.

The question of personal honour, misunderstood through so many centuries, which false interpretation has largely added to the population of graveyards, is truly stated in the Proverbs:

It is an honour for a man to cease from strife: but every fool will be meddling.

The talk of bargainers has not greatly changed.

It is naught, it is naught, saith the buyer: but when he is gone his way, then he boasteth.

One of the favourite sources of humour in the mediaeval poems and plays was a woman with a bad temper; she was represented as a terror to the most valiant man. I wonder if she was as common in real life as on the stage and in fiction? and if so, was it because her disposition was ruined by her husband? In the Proverbs, this character is repeatedly mentioned:

It is better to dwell in a corner of the housetop, than with a brawling woman in a wide house.

It is better to dwell in the wilderness, than with a contentious and an angry woman.

(Wilderness were paradise enow!)

A continual dropping in a very rainy day and a contentious woman are alike.

Many verses deal with opportune and inopportune speech; nothing seems more beautiful than just the right word spoken in just the right way at just the right time; whereas nothing is more unbearable than the fatuous presumption of those numerous babblers who seem to have a positive genius for the inopportune.

A word fitly spoken is like apples of gold in pictures of silver.

As an earring of gold, and an ornament of fine gold, so is a wise reprover upon an obedient ear.

As the cold of snow in the time of harvest, so is a faithful messenger to them that send him: for he refresheth the soul of his masters.

On the other hand:

Whoso boasteth himself of a false gift is like clouds and wind without rain. A man that beareth false witness against his neighbour is a maul, and a sword, and a sharp arrow.

Confidence in an unfaithful friend in time of trouble is like a broken tooth, and a foot out of joint.

As he that taketh away a garment in cold weather, and as vinegar upon nitre, so is he that singeth songs to an heavy heart.

He that blesseth his friend with a loud voice, rising early in the morning, it shall be counted a curse to him.

It would seem that even in those days the jovial back-slapper usually selected the wrong time for his enthusiasm. Practical jokers were also common, and were regarded with the detestation they have always deserved.

So is the man that deceiveth his neighbour, and saith: Am not I in sport?

The truly wise man not only does not trust others overmuch, he does not trust himself. Some Frenchman said that the biggest fool in the world was the man who believed he could know himself. The wisest man among the Greeks was Ulysses, whose wisdom was particularly shown in his distrust of his own heart, and the preparations he made against himself. When he had been warned that the song of the Sirens was fatal, he had the ears of his crew plugged, so that they could hear nothing, for he knew that sailors are not to be trusted with women. But his supreme wisdom was shown in the way he overreached himself, providing against his folly in advance. He wished to hear this ravishing melody, for he desired to have every possible experience; so he left his own ears unstopped, but bade the sailors tie him securely to the mast, and to pay no attention to him, if he should struggle to break loose; on no account to release him. Then when he heard the music, although he was the wisest man in the world, and had been distinctly warned of this particular danger, he struggled with all his might to be free, and cursed the sailors for disregarding his wild writhings; but he had foreseen his own danger, knew he could not trust himself, and had thus saved himself from himself. All this was clearly stated in one verse of the Proverbs:

He that trusteth in his own heart is a fool.

It should be remembered that when St. Paul, in the twelfth chapter of the Letter to the Romans, gave his famous advice to overcome an enemy with kindness, he was quoting from the old book of Proverbs:

If thine enemy be hungry, give him bread to eat; and if he be thirsty, give him water to drink:

For thou shalt heap coals of fire upon his head.

Occasionally there is a touch of mystic beauty, wise with a wisdom far beyond the wisdom of this world. It is the profound wisdom of poetry and religion.

Where there is no vision, the people perish.

Of all the chapters in Proverbs, my favourite is the thirtieth. This is said to contain the words of Agur, the son of Jakeh, being his confession of faith and the summary of his observations and knowledge of life. I wish we knew something about Agur; but he is as complete a puzzle as Melchizedek. No one knows anything either of him or his father except their names. He was a wise man, who had learned much in his way of life; he had keen eyes, an understanding heart, a fine sense of humour, and a vivid imagination.

His prayer is for neither poverty nor riches; lead me not into temptation. If I am poor, I may steal, or become morose, and blaspheme God. If I am rich, I may become self-satisfied, and worship myself instead of God. His ideal in everything is moderation, for he has observed the never-dying greediness of man, and how increase of desire brings misery.

The horseleach hath two daughters, crying: Give, give. There are three things which are never satisfied, yea, four things say not, It is enough: The grave; and the barren womb; the earth that is not filled with water; and the fire that saith not, It is enough.

The beauty and mystery of life filled his mind; he meditated often and deeply. He thought about the progress through the air of the still-winged eagle, which no one yet understands; of the swift gliding of the snake across a stone; of a ship close-hauled to the wind; and above all, of that mystery of mysteries, on which both human life and human art are founded, the relation of man to woman.

There be three things which are too wonderful for me, yea, four which I know not: The way of an eagle in the air; the way of a serpent upon a rock; the way of a ship in the midst of the sea; and the way of a man with a maid.

As he looked back on the vexations of life, he tried to think of what is most intolerable; and he decided that there were four things which cannot be borne—a servant when he reigneth, (see Kipling), a fool when he is filled with meat, an odious woman when she is married, and an handmaid that is heir to her mistress.

From these unpleasant spectacles, he turns to the contemplation of four small and weak animals, who nevertheless may teach us much.

There be four things which are little upon the earth, but they are exceeding wise:

The ants are a people not strong, yet they prepare their meat in the summer; The conies are but a feeble folk, yet make they their houses in the rocks; The locusts have no king, yet go they forth all of them by bands; The spider taketh hold with her hands, and is in kings' palaces.

The ants are not strong in body, but strong in mind; they prepare themselves against the evil day, and thus in time of distress are really stronger than giants, for they have enough. The conies were little rabbits, who had no aggressive weapons and no defence except flight; but by building their houses in the rocks, these feeble folk became just as strong as their impregnable home. The locusts learned what no community of human beings have ever yet learned, how to make their world safe for democracy; they have no tyrannical and capricious king, no written constitution, yet they understand how to govern themselves and can live and work together harmoniously; the ugly spider rises aloft, and dwells, with all her ugliness, in the splendid palace of the king. She aspired. And so these four humble creatures are illustrations to the observing Agur of four ideas: The wisdom of preparedness, the wisdom of safety, the wisdom of cooperation, and the wisdom of beauty.

The last chapter is said to contain the words of King Lemuel, who is generally believed to be no other than Solomon. It is full of deep insight, because, as we are told in the first verse, he is simply repeating what his mother taught him. She told him how to become and how to remain a wise king and a beneficent ruler; two excesses must be resolutely avoided—strange women and strong liquor. Both indulgences have destroyed innumerable kings. If it really is Solomon talking, he resembles other men in neglecting his mother's counsel. A king, she added, is also a judge, and if he drinks too much, his power of judgment is perverted, and his wisdom will be turned into folly. Use wine only as medicine, as a stimulant for those who are desperately ill, and to comfort those suffering from melancholia.

Then suddenly she passes to the consideration of that subject, which is a perennial theme—Woman.

Who is the ideal woman? What does she do? how does she dress? what does she say? Now although fashions in garments, in manners, in appearance, change bewilderingly from generation to generation, it is safe to say that the ideal woman as herein represented, will never go out of style, and will never cease to be attractive. Modesty is accompanied by the charm of mystery; character withstands the insidious decay of years; good sense is always current coin; kindness is the glory of a woman's conversation, as venomous speech is its degradation.

Who can find a virtuous woman? for her price is far above rubies. The heart of her husband doth safely trust in her, so that he shall have no need of spoil.

She will do him good and not evil all the days of her life.
She stretcheth out her hands to the poor; yea, she reacheth forth her hands to the needy.
She is not afraid of the snow for her household: for all her household are clothed with scarlet.
She maketh herself coverings of tapestry; her clothing is silk and purple.
Her husband is known in the gates, when he sitteth among the elders of the land.
Strength and honour are her clothing; and she shall rejoice in time to come.
She openeth her mouth with wisdom; and in her tongue is the law of kindness.
She looketh well to the ways of her household, and eateth not the bread of idleness.
Her children arise up, and call her blessed; her husband also, and he praiseth her.

The phrase, "She shall rejoice in time to come," when literally translated, reads: "She laughs at the time to come." She has no fear of advancing years, which strike so many women with terror; for she knows that her charm is not wholly external, and that old age will only increase it.

After so many attacks on women in the Book of Proverbs, it is inspiring to read this magnificent tribute, evidently drawn from the life. And it is well to compare this ideal woman with those who, according to Addison, spend all their time decorating that part of the head known as the outside. A pretty girl without brains is described elsewhere in these proverbs, in the following homely phrase:

As a jewel of gold in a swine's snout, so is a fair woman which is without discretion.

Let us hope that among Solomon's seven hundred wives, he found one that approached the ideal set forth by his mother.

The Book of Ecclesiastes, as we have it in the Bible, may be considered as a treatise on philosophy, just as the Proverbs are a collection of wise sayings dealing with conduct. The latter belongs to the world of action, the former to the world of thought. The philosophy represented in Ecclesiastes is Pessimism—pessimism as complete and thoroughgoing as that expressed by two other literary artists, Schopenhauer and Thomas Hardy.

It is supposed to be the conclusion about life reached by the wisest man of the world, Solomon the king, the son of David. If this be true, it is quite natural, and should call for no surprise. David was a man of action, with tremendous zest for life, who enjoyed himself thoroughly; he loved women, fighting, statesmanship, singing, dancing, good company, poetry, and music; he was too busy to be a pessimist, just as a mother of ten children seldom has nervous prostration. She hasn't the time.

Solomon asked for purely mental gifts and he received them in abundance. Big, hearty David had a thoughtful son, given to introspection and much solitary meditation. It is a modern instance. One often sees today a captain of industry, who at seventy years of age, is cheerfully active; while his son, far better educated, having begun in childhood to ask awkward questions of his parents and having received no answer, now asks them of himself.

In the English text, Solomon is called the Preacher: the Hebrew word for that is Koheleth, and therefore in modern translations and commentaries this book—with the exception of the moralising passages—is said to be the work of a man named Koheleth. The late Professor Jastrow, in his interesting version and discussion of Ecclesiastes, believed Koheleth to be an assumed name. Professor Jastrow deserves the gratitude of scholars and readers for his investigations; one must always remember, however, that the largest part of his book is conjecture, and also that his translation, however close to the Hebrew, resembles all other modern translations in its inferiority in English style to the Authorised Version.

Remember that it makes absolutely no difference whether Solomon wrote it, or some obscure preacher, or a man named Koheleth, or some other man who called himself Koheleth. The important thing is that we have a magnificent piece of literature, containing a pessimistic view of life, accompanied with religious admonition. If Solomon wrote both, well and good; with his mentality, and appetites jaded by excess, it would fit him perfectly.

In the Note-Book of the Russian novelist, Chekhov, we find this interesting monologue:

Solomon (alone). Oh! how dark is life! No night, when I was a child, so terrified me by its darkness as does my invisible existence. Lord, to David my father Thou gavest only the gift of harmonising words and sounds, to sing and praise Thee on strings, to lament sweetly, to make people weep or admire beauty; but why hast Thou given me a meditative, sleepless, hungry mind? Like an insect born of the dust, I hide in darkness; and in fear and despair, all shaking and shivering, I see and hear in everything an invisible mystery. Why this morning? Why does the sun come out from behind the temple and gild the palm tree? Why this beauty of women? Where does the bird hurry; what is the meaning of its flight, if it and its young and the place to which it hastens will, like myself, turn to dust? It were better I had never been born or were a stone, to which God has given neither eyes nor thoughts. In order to tire out my body by nightfall, all day yesterday, like a mere workman, I carried marble to the temple; but now the night has come and I cannot sleep......I'll go and lie down.

Phorsco told me that if one imagines a flock of sheep running and fixes one's attention upon it, the mind gets confused and one falls asleep. I'll do it......(Exit.)

Elsewhere Chekhov wrote in his Note-Book, "Solomon made a great mistake when he asked for wisdom."

It is interesting to observe that the English novelist, John Galsworthy, in his novel, *To Let,* has created a character whose philosophy is exactly similar to that expressed in Ecclesiastes. This man is the Belgian, Monsieur Profond, who has completely exhausted life, and has neither enthusiasm nor principles; his remark about every occupation, interest, and life itself is simply that there is nothing in it.

If Solomon wrote only the pessimism in the book of Ecclesiastes, and some pious scribe added the religious admonitions, very well; they are both true, taken separately or together. Without any faith in God, life ceases to have any meaning, which is precisely the view taken in the body of the text; with faith in God, even the sorrows of life have significance, because everything has a meaning, which is the view taken by the commentator.

Therefore it is not surprising to find this book in the Bible. The objections to it as a portion of Holy Writ are based on the fact that it expresses pessimism and despair; but it does not teach pessimism and despair. Jezebel expresses in her life, conduct, and talk a certain kind of woman; but she is not meant to be a model.

The Book of Ecclesiastes is one of the most modern of all the sixty-six parts of the Bible— because pessimism is to-day an extremely popular attitude of mind. One reason why pessimism is popular is because the majority of people have the insidious taint of self-pity, and imagine that their particular troubles are more severe than those carried by others. Furthermore, a great many have lost all religious faith and with it the key to life; life is certainly a mystery to all of us, but to some it is a marvellous and challenging mystery, to others a hopeless and purpose-crushing puzzle. One man rises higher by reason of an obstacle; another is tripped by it, never to rise again.

It is also characteristic that modern critics like the pessimism of this book better than the religious teaching it contains; for many would much rather be told what a wretched time they are having, poor fellows, than to be told how to improve the situation—especially when the latter plan means real work.

It is often said that the Preacher is like Omar Khayyam; so he is, if you leave out the *practical* philosophies of both. Omar says that we know not whence we came nor whither we are going; therefore, take a drink. This book says we know nothing about life, therefore fear God and keep His commandments.

Personally, I have never been able to see why ignorance of life should produce a thirst. I suppose that what is meant, is to drug one's puzzled mind into oblivion, so that one can forget the mystery of life. Now inasmuch as mind is the best thing we have, I prefer to keep it as clear as possible. A tiny candle may not go far in the darkness, but it is better than more darkness.

It is a curious fact that people who are sick, or poor, or crippled are not as a rule pessimists; the pessimists are recruited from the ranks of the healthy and wealthy, who have grown dull from easily satisfied desires.

The Preacher loses no time in stating his philosophical position. His first word is Vanity—*vanitas vanitatum*. There is nothing new under the sun. Generations come and go, and the earth abideth forever. The Preacher had seen everything, had tasted all experience, had eaten freely of the tree of knowledge, and had come to this conclusion— there is nothing in it! Life is meaningless. Observe that, like a genuine philosophical pessimist, he does not lay the main emphasis on the sorrows and discomforts of life; for these could be borne, bad as they are, if we knew we were going somewhither, if we knew pain had a meaning. Real pessimism rises not from experience of pain, but from the fear that life is without significance. Nothing makes any difference. Oblivion swallows us all. He hated life, with that common and yet peculiar fallacy of thought; he hated life, because he hated death. If life is hateful, death should be welcome; if life is wretched, its shortness should be counted as an asset; but in reality nobody loves life deep down in his heart like your pessimist—whose two reasons for hating life are first, that it is short, and second, that it is followed by oblivion.

Then said I in my heart, As it happeneth to the fool, so it happeneth even to me; and why was I then more wise? Then I said in my heart, that this also is vanity.

For there is no remembrance of the wise more than of the fool forever; seeing that which now is in the days to come shall all be forgotten. And how dieth the wise man? As the fool.

Therefore I hated life; because the work that is wrought under the sun is grievous unto me: for all is vanity and vexation; of spirit.

Later, this hater of life reveals his love of it,, which explains what I mean by saying that no one loves life like your pessimist.

For to him that is joined to all the living there is hope: for a living dog is better than a dead lion.

For the living know that they shall die: but the dead know not any thing, neither have they any more a reward; for the memory of them is forgotten. Also their love, and their hatred, and their envy, is now perished; neither have they any more a portion for ever in any thing that is done under the sun.

One of his statements, which is constantly quoted, is certainly not true: "Increase of knowledge in-creaseth sorrow." One might as well say that the view at the base of a tower is finer than the view from the top thereof; or that one leg is better than two. Although the famous assertion of the Preacher is false, his philosophy is consistently founded upon it; youth is the best time of life and old age the most miserable. The noble poetry of the book, which in the Authorised Version, is full of solemn and mournful music, reaches its splendid climax in the last chapter; the language of despair has never reached elsewhere such an elevation as in this lamentation on old age, where one hardly knows which to admire more, the language or the rhythm; the swiftly following succession of vivid metaphors, or the swelling adagio music:

While the evil days come not, nor the years draw nigh, when thou shalt say, I have no pleasure in them;

While the sun, or the light, or the moon, or the stars, be not darkened, nor the clouds return after the rain:

In the day when the keepers of the house shall tremble, and the strong men shall bow themselves, and the grinders cease because they are few, and those that look out of the windows be darkened.

The keepers of the house are either the ribs or the hips; the strong men are the legs; the grinders are the molars; the windows are the eyes, and the sight is dim with advancing years.

And the doors shall be shut in the streets, when the sound of the grinding is low, and he shall rise up at the voice of the bird, and all the daughters of musick shall be brought low.

The doors are the ears, which age closes up; the sound of the grinding is low presumably means that penetrating noises reach old ears dim and muffled; he shall rise up at the voice of the bird—one of the all but universal accompaniments of old age is inability to sleep late in the morning; in the days of Ecclesiastes, as now, the old man woke at

The earliest pipe of half-awakened bird

and wondered how he would get through the three hours before breakfast. The daughters of music shall be brought low does not mean that the voice will be of lower register, for in the only passage fit to be compared with this, the soliloquy of Jaques in *As You Like It,* he has the manly voice change into thin, childish treble; what it means is that the music of health will leave the voice of old age, which will have no vibration, but will be thin and unpleasant; the daughters of music are slain.

Also when they shall be afraid of that which is high, and fears shall be in the way, and the almond tree shall flourish, and the grasshopper shall be a burden, and desire shall fail.

Fear of that which is high means that old age does not like hills, not even stairs; fears shall be in the way refers to the timidity that accompanies the old man in every movement; the almond tree has white blossoms, referring to the white hair; the grasshopper shall be a burden probably means simply that even the merest trifle causes worry; desire refers to the loss of virility.

Because man goeth to his long home, and the mourners go about the streets: Or ever the silver cord be loosed, or the golden bowl be broken, or the pitcher be broken at the fountain, or the wheel broken at the cistern.

The funeral processions in the streets mean more to an old man than to youth, being a kind of public rehearsal of his own tragedy; the silver cord may be the spine, and the golden bowl the head, containing the brain, which has lost its activity; what is meant by the pitcher and the wheel nobody knows; Professor Jastrow thinks they may refer to the kidneys and intestines. But they may mean simply the inability of the old man to carry out any plan; at the very moment of action, his purpose is made sterile by weakness, as the pitcher is broken just when you want to fill it, and the wheel broken at just the time when you need its revolution.

Vanity of vanities, saith the preacher; all is vanity.

    Last scene of all,
That ends this strange, eventful history,
Is second childishness and mere oblivion;
Sans teeth, sans eyes, sans taste, sans everything.

Which speech Shakespeare put into the mouth of an idle and disillusioned spectator, as the Bible places similar views in the mouth of a tired and jaded king.

The commentator could not let such philosophy pass without an antidote; just as a physician gives a remedy for disease, so this commentator, whether he were the original philosopher or some one who had read the despairing words with curiosity and dissent, added very sensibly:

This is the conclusion of the whole matter; fear God and keep His commandments.

Or, as Tennyson says,

Hold thou the good; define it well
    For fear divine Philosophy
    Should push beyond her mark, and be
Procuress to the Lords of Hell.

XII

HUMAN NATURE REVEALED IN POETRY

JOB, SOLOMON'S SONG, PSALMS, ISAIAH

Variety of Literary Forms in the Book of Job—The Opening Scene—Problem of Evil—Character of Job—Bad News— Satan's Technique—Effect of Bodily Pain on the Mind—The Boils—The Three Friends—Their Speeches and Job's Replies—His Exasperation—Job's Remarks on Death—The Question in Job, and the Answer in John—Job's Appeal to Posterity—Job's Long Apology for His Life—An Outbreak from the Younger Generation—Conceit, Assurance, and Verbosity of Elihu—God's Patience Exhausted—The Voice Out of the Whirlwind—Sublime Figures—Humility of Job—His Final Prosperity—Passionate Love in Solomon's Song—The Lyrics in the Psalms—The Twenty-third Psalm and Its Influence— Hunger and Thirst for Righteousness—Security in God—The Imprecatory Psalms and the Sermons Preached During the Great War—Solemn Grandeur of the Ninetieth Psalm—Length of Life—Philosophy of Life—The Modern Attitude—Hotspur and Roosevelt—God's Search for Man—Patriotic Psalms— Isaiah's Passion for Right Conduct—His Attack on the Leaders of the Church—His Prophecy of Ultimate Triumph Through the Coming of Jesus Christ.

The Book of Job is a work of pure literature; it is a pastoral, it is a novel, it is a philosophical treatise in the form of a dialogue, it is a drama, and above all it is a poem. It is animated throughout by the very spirit of poetry—it is indeed one of the greatest poems of the world. As a pastoral, it deals with the land and possessions of a rich stock farmer; as a novel, it contains incidents so interesting that, once read, they are never forgotten; as philosophy, it deals with one of the most important problems, the significance of pain, and leaves us where all other treatises on this subject have left us, in the dark; as a drama, it has action and talk, both so appealing that when it was presented on the New York stage it had a long run; as poetry, it reaches the highest elevations known to the human spirit, and loses itself in the stars.

It has everything except one thing—love o' women. Curious, that a narrative-pastoral-philo-sophical-dramatic-poem can be so thrilling without making any use of the chief material for all these forms of literature.

It opens in the liveliest fashion, so lively that Goethe borrowed it for the opening of *Faust*. Job had that combination of piety and wealth so often exemplified in the town's leading citizen. He sought first the kingdom of God and His righteousness, and all these other things were added unto him. Thus Satan sneered, as some of the ungodly do to-day, whenever Job was held up as an illustration of religion. It is easy to be good when you have plenty of money and good health—take these away and faith in God will have wings like riches and fly.

So far as the problem of evil is concerned, it is interesting to notice that Satan spent his time traveling, going freely hither and thither, and was given a free hand. Thus the Spirit of Opposition, the Spirit of Negation, the Super-Mischief-maker was and apparently is eternally busy, and could point with pride to his solid accomplishments.

God and Satan fought for the soul of Job, as they fight for every human being; apparently even the meanest is worth fighting for. No one has ever got any further with the doctrine of predestination than the coloured preacher who said, "God predestines man to be saved: the Devil predestines man to be damned; and man has the casting vote."

Satan was allowed to try his technique on Job's prosperity and security. Four servants came running in turn to Job, bringing him news of disaster: the first spoke of robbers, who had destroyed property and servants; the second, of lightning destroying sheep and shepherds; the third, of three bands of marauders who stole all the camels and killed their drivers; the fourth, of a cyclone which destroyed the manor house and killed his seven sons.

Job received these four blows with that equanimity that accompanies only the most steadfast faith. He worshipped God, who had given and taken away: blessed be the name of the Lord.

When Satan appeared again before the Most High, he did not look like a defeated antagonist; he was reminded that Job's piety had not been lessened or stained by disaster. Satan suggested that there was one thing that no faith could overcome—physical suffering. It will be remembered that in *In Memoriam* we read,

Be near me when the sensuous frame
Is rack'd with pangs that conquer trust,

It is unfortunate that just when faith should be brightest it is often most dim—

in times of bodily anguish. When the body is racked with pain, religion should help to fortify the mind; but it is just then when religious feeling is often dominated and driven from the field by corporal discomfort. Shakespeare intimated that there was no philosophy proof against toothache; and it is true that until a philosopher can get the tooth fixed or removed, he is not likely to make any valuable contribution to human thought. No saying is more vain than to say that extreme pain stimulates and exalts the mind; it really stupefies one's thinking powers, and for the very simple reason that pain is so all-pervading that there is no room in the mind for anything else. Suddenly Job's portly body was embossed with boils; he could neither stand, nor sit, nor lie down with any comfort. His wife mocked his faith, and advised him to curse God and die. You see, don't you, how far you have got with religion? Perhaps she wanted to get rid of him. He must have been rather trying in the days of his health and prosperity; for there is only one husband more exasperating than an impatient one, and that is one who is patient. And what a sight he was now! Job rebuked her sharply for blasphemy, told her that we receive both good and evil from God, and must not expect continual fine weather. Up to this moment he had uttered nothing in rebellion or in despair; and it is just possible that his faith might have withstood even the boils if his three friends had not taken it into their heads to visit and console him. I say he might have triumphed over either the boils or the friends; but the combination was too much, even for Job, and he cursed his birthday. It was quite evident to the sufferer, as he saw the three approaching, with their faces properly adjusted for sympathy, that there was team-play here; they had evidently talked him over and made an appointment to visit him. Had he known the poetry of Browning he might have cried out to them:

Has some plague a longer lease,
   Proffering its help uncouth?
Can't one even die in peace?

He recognised them afar off, but he was so changed from the prosperous, upstanding, hearty man that at first they did not know him; when his identity finally became clear, they were so overcome as to be speechless seven days and seven nights. His appearance must have produced a terrific shock to silence such fluency as theirs.

The seven days of silence were broken by the voice of Job, who uttered a noble psalm in praise of Death; his condition and the words springing from it take us back to those two wonderful verses in Ecclesiasticus, cited in a previous chapter—how bitter the thought of death is when one is healthy and prosperous, how welcome when one is in anguish, and especially when one "hath lost patience." Job exemplified this changing attitude in the change of his own condition.

Eliphaz cleared his throat, and began somewhat doubtfully, "If we assay to commune with thee, wilt thou be grieved?" He reminded Job that no man was perfect, hence every one needs refinement by suffering; he advised him not to despise the chastening of the Almighty, but to have faith that he would come out of this trial a sounder and better man. But Job answered that the arrows of the Almighty had pierced him; that he was in such grief he longed believe that he was being punished for sin. He challenged Eliphaz to point out wherein he had gone wrong.

Then Bildad the Shuhite spoke up, rather vaguely, it must be confessed: he referred to history, as proving that the righteous prosper and the wicked suffer, which, if he had known a little more history, he might have urged with less assurance; he practically told Job to cheer up, for he would surely be all right again, though he did not suggest when or how.

To this Job made the reply that millions have made in suffering; how am I to establish an intimate relation with the great God? Does He hold court like a human judge, so that I can stand before Him and present my case? How can I get a hearing? How can I be sure that He, who made Arcturus, Orion, and the Pleiades, cares anything for me, any more than I care for a worm? No, it is not because I have sinned that I am punished; I don't know why I suffer so; all I want now is a little respite before death, the end of consciousness, the end of pain.

Wherefore then hast thou brought me forth out of the womb? Oh that I had given up the ghost, and no eye had seen me!

I should have been as though I had not been; I should have been carried from the womb to the grave.

Are not my days few? Cease then, and let me alone, that I may take comfort a little,

Before I go whence I shall not return, even to the land of darkness and the shadow of death;

A land of darkness, as darkness itself; and of the shadow of death, without any order, and where the light is as darkness.

Many poets have attempted to express the idea of nothingness; Shakespeare spoke of death's dateless night: Job, a distinguished man of business, with definite plans for each day, calls the land of the dead a place "without any order."

Then the third friend, Zophar the Naamathite, who had thus far kept silent with great difficulty, burst out in a torrent of speech, hotly condemning Job for self-righteousness. He called upon him to repent, and all might yet be well. Who can know the infinite mind? who by searching can find out God? Therefore, Job, I advise you to humble yourself in the dust, put away your sins, and repent; then all will be forgiven, and you will remember these boils only as a bad dream.

Job was decidedly irritated by the words of Zophar, and answered sarcastically, "No doubt but ye are the people, and wisdom shall die with you." (On the stage this line was spoken with such an indescribable tone of mingled wrath, impatience, and suffering that the audience burst out in uncontrollable laughter.) He went on to say that he too was not devoid of understanding; compared with God, he was nothing; but compared with his three friends, he felt no inferiority in intellect; my neighbours are mocking me; it is easy to talk when you are feeling fine yourself.

But ye are forgers of lies, ye are all physicians of no value.
O that ye would altogether hold your peace, and it should be your wisdom.

The fact is that God does not need such persons as you to speak in His behalf; you cannot understand His ways; He does not always punish the wicked, and help the good. There is no formula.

The truth is that life is nothing but vanity and sorrow, as meaningless as death. Then out of the depths Job asks the eternal question: Is there any better life than this miserable existence? Is there any reason for hope in a life after death, where our dreams of perfection may reach fulfillment? As the best answer to this question was made by Him who spake as never man spake, I wish to place together question and answer—the question in the fourteenth chapter of Job, the answer in the fourteenth chapter of John. The answer is as refreshing as clear water to thirst, as healing balm to a painful wound.

THE QUESTION

Man that is born of a woman is of few days, and full of trouble.
He cometh forth like a flower, and is cut down: he fleeth also as a shadow, and continueth not. .....
For there is hope of a tree, if it be cut down, that it will sprout again, and that the tender branch thereof will not cease......
But man dieth, and wasteth away: yea, man giveth up the ghost, and where is he?.....
If a man die, shall he live again?

THE ANSWER

Let not your heart be troubled: ye believe in God, believe also in me.

In my Father's house are many mansions: if it were not so, I would have told you. I go to prepare a place for you.

The three friends were neither silenced nor convinced by Job's speeches; Eliphaz the Temanite began again, and said that Job had filled his belly with the east wind. He declared that it was not only foolish but wicked to ask questions of God, or to suggest that He was not dealing fairly by the world. Like the other two, he could not get the idea of sin and punishment out of his head, and rebuked the sufferer.

Job's original stock of patience was now quite exhausted. "Miserable comforters are ye all." I appeal from you to my Witness in heaven; for although my anguish comes from Him, He understands me, and you do not. Your words are merely an addition to an already intolerable burden.

Bildad the Shuhite, having the sensitiveness that sometimes accompanies vanity, sharply resented these amenities, and interrupted Job by telling him to keep still and listen to words of wisdom. He then poured out another diatribe on the wicked, predicting disaster for those who would not repent. Job told Bildad that he ought to be ashamed of himself for such talk, for it had no friendliness nor understanding. Can't you see that while you are delivering these discourses, I am suffering horribly?

Have pity upon me, have pity upon me, O ye my friends; for the hand of God hath touched me.

Then follows an interesting remark, which (as the late Professor Jastrow pointed out) has been almost universally misunderstood. Job here appeals from his contemporaries, who scorn him, to future time—indeed, to us in the twentieth century —when some defender will appear who will do him justice. Like many a man who suffers from misrepresentation, he appeals to posterity. When he said, "I know that my Redeemer liveth," he apparently was not referring to Christ nor to Jehovah; the word Redeemer should have been translated defender—and Job means, if only my suffering could be recorded in a book, some wise man in the future would read it, and defend me against the reproaches of Eliphaz, Bildad, and Zophar

Oh that my words were now written! Oh that they were printed in a book! That they were graven with an iron pen and lead in the rock for ever! For I know that my Redeemer liveth, and that He shall stand at the latter day upon the earth.

His pious wish has been fulfilled. We understand Job better, and the homiletic fury of the three friends is almost as irritating to us as it was to him.

While Professor Jastrow has done much to stimulate thought on this great poem, he went altogether too far in reconstructing the work, in an attempt to make it consistent. Who expects the lamentations of one who was in such acute misery as Job to form a consistent doctrine or to maintain the same attitude toward life and death? At times he speaks in utter despair, and again with some hope, as any man would in changing moods.

Sometimes he believes in a future life, at other times not at all, as is the way of fluctuating human opinion.

Zophar the Naamathite, like a bird with one tune, poured some more hot words into the wicked, who, he informed Job, might triumph temporarily, but in the end would receive their deserts. Look out.

Job replied, in the tone of a man who knows that what he will say will produce no conviction, yet must speak.

Suffer me that I may speak; and after that I have spoken, mock on.

He said that while it was true that some of the wicked suffered, some of them did not; if you will look on life as it is, without any preconceived theory, you will see that your explanation of human suffering does not fit the facts. In this speech Job really took the same position as that declared many years later by our Lord: He sendeth His rain on the just and on the unjust.

Eliphaz, however, resembled many philosophers in loving his theory more than the truth. He told Job to look back over his entire career, and he would certainly remember many things he had done which were not right; *hinc illæ lachrimæ.*

Ah, said Job, if only I knew where I might find God, to be as sure of Him as you are; if only I could ask Him a few questions, and know the explanation of life I The world is full of evil, and God permits murderers and adulterers to live. If I were God, I might know why.

Bildad, whose ammunition was nearly all exhausted, here fired a shot aimed apparently at no target; man, he said, must not attempt to justify himself. Job then made a very long speech, full of disconnected remarks, many of which contain beautiful figures of speech, but have little to do with the argument. He talks like a man who is afraid to stop for fear his antagonist will begin again, and he had rather talk than listen. He reviewed his former happy life, and contrasted it with his present wretched state.

When he finished, it was Zophar's turn; but he said nothing. Perhaps he was asleep. Job's speech was very long.

But there was a young man, Elihu the Buzite, who had been listening, and was by this time angry with both sides; with Job, because he had attempted to justify himself, and with the three comforters, because they were silenced; really, however, he was angry because he had been bursting with repressed rhetoric, and had not got a chance to put in a word. He released a flood of talk—his conceit, so characteristic of the younger generation, is downright funny.

I will answer also my part, I also will shew mine opinion.
For I am full of matter, the spirit within me constraineth me.
Behold, my belly is as wine which hath no vent; it is ready to burst like new bottles.
I will speak, that I may be refreshed; I will open my lips and answer.

He was in terror lest Job should interrupt him before he got through; never was there a man who more loved to hear himself talk. After he had been pouring out a steady torrent of words, it is evident that Job made an attempt to speak, and Elihu cried hastily:

Mark well, O Job, hearken unto me: hold thy peace, and I will speak.
If thou hast anything to say, answer me: speak, for I desire to justify thee.
If not, hearken unto me: hold thy peace, and I shall teach thee wisdom.

Job was too amazed to speak, and Elihu went on endlessly, until he had exhausted not only the patience of Job, but the patience of God.

The wind of Elihu had brought on a whirlwind, and out of the storm came a great Voice, with language majestic and divine:

Who is this that darkeneth counsel by words without knowledge? Gird up now thy loins like a man; for I will demand of thee, and answer thou me.

Where wast thou when I laid the foundations of the earth? declare, if thou hast understanding......
Whereupon are the foundations thereof fastened, or who laid the corner stone thereof;
When the morning stars sang together, and all the sons of God shouted for joy?
Or who shut up the sea with doors, when it brake forth, as if it had issued out of the womb?
When I made the cloud the garment thereof, and thick darkness a swaddlingband for it,
And brake up for it my decreed place, and set bars and doors,
And said, Hitherto shalt thou come, but no further: and here shall thy proud waves be stayed......

Canst thou bind the sweet influences of Pleiades, or loose the bands of Orion? Canst thou bring forth Mazzaroth in his season? or canst thou guide Arcturus with his sons?.....

Hast thou given the horse strength? hast thou clothed his neck with thunder? Canst thou make him afraid as a grasshopper? the glory of his nostrils is terrible.

He paweth in the valley, and rejoiceth in his strength: he goeth on to meet the armed men.

He mocketh at fear, and is not affrighted; neither turneth he back from the sword.

The quiver rattleth against him, the glittering spear and the shield.

He swalloweth the ground with fierceness and rage: neither believeth he that it is the sound of the trumpet.

He saith among the trumpets, Ha, ha; and he smelleth the battle afar off, the thunder of the captains, and the shouting......

This glorious poetry, setting forth the wonders of the earth, and of the starry heavens, indicated the distance between the mind of man and the mind of God. Job, who had maintained an attitude of defiance to his three friends, and doubtless an attitude of bewilderment to Elihu, now humbled himself in the presence of the works of God. "I abhor myself, and repent in dust and ashes."

Eliphaz and his two friends received a merited rebuke from the divine voice, and were informed that their wisdom was all foolishness; but Job would pray for them, that their presumption might be forgiven. They were sadder and wiser for this experience, and prepared a burnt offering.

Job forgave them, and it is pleasant to observe that at the moment when he prayed for his old friends, his boils left him, and he was clean. Prosperity returned to him abundantly, his sons grew apace, and his daughters were the fairest women in the land. He lived one hundred and forty years after his memorable misfortune, and greeted his great-grandchildren.

What Satan thought of all this is not recorded; but the problem of evil is left just where it was before the discussion, just where every philosopher leaves it when he has said his last word.

The Song of Songs, called Solomon's Song, is a collection of passionate Eastern lyrics dealing with love, courtship and marriage. It is rather curious that this very human poem, with its frank expression of desire and longing, should ever have been given a spiritual interpretation. It is like a garden; it has the roses of love and the weeds of jealousy.

The main theme is the worship of bodily beauty; the richly ornamental and odorous words take the form of a duet, in which the maiden and the man sing alternately in praise of the other's charms. The girl looks shyly out through the lattice and sees with adoration the approaching figure of her lover running to meet her, full of vigour, agility and grace. He is like a young hart, leaping on the mountains. To the passionate eyes of the man, the maiden is as a fair lily among thistles, and he takes delight in her slender, supple sweetness.

Journeys end in lovers meeting; it is the union of youth in springtime. Surely no song to the freshness of spring ever surpassed this:

For, lo, the winter is past, the rain is over and gone;
The flowers appear on the earth; the time of the singing of birds is come, and the voice of the turtle is heard in our land;
The fig tree putteth forth her green figs, and the vines with the tender grape give a good smell. Arise, my love, my fair one, and come away......
My beloved is mine, and I am his; he feedeth among the lilies.

The Song celebrates not only the joy and glory of Love and Beauty, but also the Terror—for Love and Beauty may be as terrible as they are sweet.

Who is she that looketh forth as the morning, fair as the moon, clear as the sun, and terrible as an army with banners? .....

Set me as a seal upon thine heart, as a seal upon thine arm: for love is strong as death; jealousy is cruel as the grave: the coals thereof are coals of fire, which hath a most vehement flame.

Many waters cannot quench love, neither can the floods drown it: if a man would give all the substance of his house for love, it would utterly be contemned.

The Book of Psalms contains one hundred and fifty lyrical poems. A true lyric should have three distinct qualities—brevity, melody, unity. By its very nature it must be brief; we can enjoy a long narrative or descriptive poem, but a long lyric would be as intolerable as a long tune. A lyrical poem should be fluently musical, singing spontaneously; and it should as a rule represent only one mood. This mood may not be characteristic of the author's usual mental attitude, but it is his feeling at the time when he finds relief in expression.

The one apparent exception to the rule of brevity is Psalm CXIX; but that is a group of songs, rather than one.

Divine lyrics have never reached a loftier height than in the Psalms, which is the greatest Hymn Book in the world. Almost every human emotion— except the love of man and woman—is represented. In this correspondence with God there is an intimate revelation of the human heart, a marvellous confessional. There are songs of joy, triumph, hate, rage, fear, repentance, remorse, praise, adoration, ecstasy, and despair. There is the fierce tumult of battle, there is the quiet tone of serene meditation. The works of nature are the handiwork of God; there is the glory of the morning, the glory of the evening, and the glory of the stars. Often the writer sings as intimately and unrestrainedly as though he were alone with God.

There are only six verses in the Twenty-third Psalm, but who can estimate the range and extent of their heart-strengthening influence? Thousands and thousands have gone through pain, sorrow, humiliation, and death with these immortal words on their lips. They have literally restored the soul of sufferers. In the universality of their import and application they belong to all people and all time.

The Lord is my shepherd; I shall not want.
He maketh me to lie down in green pastures: he leadeth me beside the still waters.
He restoreth my soul: he leadeth me in the paths of righteousness for his name's sake.
Yea, though I walk through the valley of the shadow of death, I will fear no evil: for thou art with me; thy rod and thy staff they comfort me.
Thou preparest a table before me in the presence of mine enemies: thou anointest my head with oil; my cup runneth over.
Surely goodness and mercy shall follow me all the days of my life: and I will dwell in the house of the Lord for ever.

Those who are not religious, who never think of religion subjectively, have no more idea of the reality of religious passion than those who have never been in love have a conception of the power of love; they understand the ardour of religion as a deaf man understands music and a man born blind appreciates a sunset. In Psalm XLII the poet expresses a feeling instantly understood by some, and meaningless to others:

As the hart panteth after the water brooks, so panteth my soul after thee, O God.
My soul thirsteth for God, for the living God: when shall I come and appear before God?

The innumerable hosts of those who have lived the life of the spirit and found in that life solid and unshakable security feel in their hearts an echo to the majestic opening of the Forty-sixth Psalm:

God is our refuge and strength, a very present help in trouble.
Therefore will not we fear, though the earth be removed, and though the mountains be carried into the midst of the sea;
Though the waters thereof roar and be troubled, though the mountains shake with the swelling thereof.

In recent times, up to the year of grace 1914, many godly people were troubled by the so-called imprecatory psalms, where the poets called on God to torture, crush, and annihilate their enemies; these psalms were written by fighters, who hated their enemies and believed that their personal enemies were the enemies of righteousness. They therefore called loudly for divine vengeance, and rejoiced in their foes' discomfiture and ruin. I say that these poems were prudently omitted from pulpit reading, as it was felt that in modern and more peaceful days we had outgrown such rancorous hostility, or at all events that we ought to have done so. But when I remember the language used in the pulpits of some American churches during the World War, I find it very easy to understand the mood of the cursing psalms, and I find it impossible to take toward those hymns of hate a superior attitude; for surely the twentieth century, as often represented by official religion, was in precisely the same frame of mind. Human nature at any critical moment may burst through the confining garments of culture, education, and religion, as an angry man throws off restraint.

This is the vigorous fashion in which the Psalmist preached in time of war; of course he believed that his own advancement and that of the Kingdom of God were firmly united; it was a holy war:

They compassed me about also with words of hatred; and fought against me without a cause......
Let his children be fatherless, and his wife a widow.
Let his children be continually vagabonds, and beg: let them seek their bread also out of their desolate places.
Let the extortioner catch all that he hath; and let the strangers spoil his labour.
Let there be none to extend mercy unto him: neither let there be any to favour his fatherless children.
Let his posterity be cut off; and in the generation following let their name be blotted out.
Let the iniquity of his fathers be remembered with the Lord; and let not the sin of his mother be blotted out.

On the night of 22 January, 1922, a clergyman in Leeds, England, made a sensation by announcing that this Psalm, CIX, would henceforth be expurgated from the service; he added that he would like also to remove Psalms XXXV and LXIX, on the ground that all three were unchristian. They are certainly unchristian, but they are not unnatural. The clergyman said, "No one has been able to explain the curses in the Psalms and they represent human nature at its very worst." Well, they represented human nature very well not only in David's time, but in 1914-18, and expressed a common feeling.

For solemn grandeur there is perhaps no poem in literature superior to the Ninetieth Psalm, believed to be one of the oldest in the book, and formerly ascribed to Moses. It could not have been written by Moses, I suppose, because it speaks of the age of man, seventy years with an occasional extension to eighty, as being normal; whereas in the early days of Jewish history a much longer life was often recorded, Moses himself dying at the age of one hundred and twenty.

The comparison of the eternal Present of God with the transient hills, and with the swift change from future to past in the life of men, is overwhelming in its stern dignity of expression. We think in hours and days, measurements adapted to our range; with Him a thousand years are but as yesterday when it is past, and as a watch in the night. This psalm is like a symphony, beginning sonorously, then descending into a mournful adagio, and closing jubilantly.

I suppose there could not be a more well-worn platitude than to say that life is short; but in our philosophical thinking we actually do forget the relativity of measurement. We measure cloth by yards, but the astronomer measures by light-years; if with God a thousand years are as a watch in the night, why are we so confident as to the goodness or the badness of the world? If a man thinks in centuries, his view is surely different from that of a child, who thinks only of to-day; how about One who thinks in terms of eternity?

On the other hand, the literature of melancholy is too much obsessed with the shortness of life; compared with the life of a California tree, human existence on earth is short indeed; but it is really long enough to enjoy greatly and to suffer greatly; long enough to do much good and much evil; long enough to learn some things well; in many strange characters, long enough to be tired of it; long enough for ennui. For there are many who would kill time, and there are occasions when to the most active mind an hour seems long.

Life may be short, as many who have wasted it find out at its close; but certainly most of us live as long as we deserve.

Hell was the first important element in theology to become discredited in modern thought; there are, of course, many who still believe in hell, but the majority of Protestant Christians probably do not. With the extinction of this flame, the fear of a future life, the dread of something after death, vanished; the future life has ceased to terrify most intelligent persons. But with the fear of the future banished, the hope of the future began to grow weak; the material expansion of modern life, followed by the World War, which calamity had a disastrous effect on religious faith—how disastrous no one now can tell—drove out of the minds of many people the hope of existence after death. The result is that there are now probably a larger number of people who have no belief in a future life than have ever existed hitherto; thus we see all about us to-day a common attitude toward this present life that can best be characterised by the word *greedy*.

Everyone seems to be afraid he will miss something ; this is the last drink, youth is fleeting, opportunity will not knock again. We behold an all but universal mad rush for "happiness," with little care for cost or consequences.

To a student of human nature, it is always interesting to see how the same premise will in different minds be followed by opposite conclusions. Omar Khayyam never had so many followers as now; life is short, therefore eat and drink, for to-morrow we die. But there are other men who, with the same prospect, come to precisely opposite ways of conduct. Life is short, therefore do as much good as possible; life is short, therefore do as much permanent work as possible, for to-morrow we die. The night cometh, when no man can work.

The gallant knight, Harry Hotspur, spoke as follows:

O gentlemen, the time of life is short;
To spend that shortness basely were too long,
If life did ride upon a dial's point,
Still ending at the arrival of an hour.

Theodore Roosevelt, the American Hotspur, in a letter to Bellamy Storer, wrote:

We have got but one life here, and what comes after it we cannot with certainty tell; but it pays, no matter what comes after it, to try and do things, to accomplish things in this life, and not merely to have a soft and pleasant time.

Psalm CIV is a swelling chorus of praise to God, in which the individual voices, earth and sky and sea, with beasts and birds and fishes, combine in majestic harmonies:

O Lord my God, thou art very great; thou art clothed with honour and majesty.
Who coverest thyself with light as with a garment; who stretchest out the heavens like a curtain:
Who layeth the beams of his chambers in the waters: who maketh the clouds his chariot: who walketh upon the wings of the wind......
He sendeth the springs into the valleys, which run among the hills......
By them shall the fowls of the heaven have their habitation, which sing among the branches......
He appointeth the moon for seasons: the sun knoweth his going down.
Thou makest darkness, and it is night: wherein all the beasts of the forest do creep forth.
The young lions roar after their prey, and seek their meat from God.

The sun ariseth, they gather themselves together, and lay them down in their dens.

Man goeth forth unto his work and to his labour until the evening.
O Lord, how manifold are thy works; in wisdom hast thou made them all: the earth is full of Thy riches.
So is this great and wide sea, wherein are things creeping innumerable, both small and great beasts.
There go the ships: there is that leviathan, whom thou hast made to play therein......
The glory of the Lord shall endure for ever: the Lord shall rejoice in his works.
He looketh on the earth, and it trembleth: he toucheth the hills, and they smoke.
I will sing unto the Lord as long as I live: I will sing praise to my God while I have my being.
My meditation of him shall be sweet: I will be glad in the Lord.

In every man's heart there is the love of his native land; and this passion is never so strong as when he is in a far country, for the bonds that unite him to his home are elastic, pulling harder as the distance increases. Nor does anyone love his country so much as when it has been defeated in war; victorious people are proud of their nation, and of their nation's flag; but their pride is not so strong as the passionate love of country among those that have been overthrown and cast down. Imagine yourself, if you can, an exile, a captive in a strange, hostile, and powerful land, suddenly seeing your own country's flag, or hearing its national song. Your feelings could never find better expression than in the Psalm CXXXVII:

By the rivers of Babylon, there we sat down, yea, we wept, when we remembered Zion.
We hanged our harps upon the willows in the midst thereof.
For there they that carried us away captive required of us a song; and they that wasted us required of us mirth, saying, Sing us one of the songs of Zion.
How shall we sing the Lord's song in a strange land?
If I forget thee, O Jerusalem, let my right hand forget her cunning.
If I do not remember thee, let my tongue cleave to the roof of my mouth; if I prefer not Jerusalem above my chief joy.

The true mystic believes that the Divine Presence is all about him; that man's search for God does not compare in eager intensity with God's search for man. For there are those who seek God in vain, when all that is needed is surrender. Children do not go out looking for their parents; they go out sometimes trying vainly to escape from the all-embracing, searching parental love. If the appearance of Jesus Christ on earth means anything, it means that the love of God is pursuing the flying heart of man. The great poet, Francis Thompson, expressed this fundamental religious idea in his extraordinary masterpiece,

The Hound of Heaven; but even his genius does not compare in truth and beauty with the inspiration and language of the one hundred and thirty-ninth Psalm:

O Lord, thou hast searched me, and known me.
Thou knowest my downsitting and mine uprising, thou un-derstandest my thought afar off.
Thou compassest my path and my lying down, and art acquainted with all my ways.

For there is not a word in my tongue, but, lo, O Lord, thou knowest it altogether.
Thou hast beset me behind and before, and laid thine hand upon me.
Such knowledge is too wonderful for me; it is high; I cannot attain unto it.
Whither shall I go from thy spirit? or whither shall I flee from thy presence?
If I ascend up into heaven, thou art there: if I make my bed in hell, behold, thou art there.
If I take the wings of the morning, and dwell in the uttermost parts of the sea;
Even there shall thy hand lead me, and thy right hand shall hold me.

In the book of the prophet Isaiah, we find not only the heights of poetry—both sublimity and tenderness—we find a revelation of the wickedness of human nature and the only remedy. In the very first chapter there is a hearty condemnation of mere church-going, formal prayers, hollow ritualistic observances, days and times of sacrifice; what is needed is regeneration, a new heart. It is an interesting comment on human nature that every truly great religious teacher has found it necessary to attack the leaders of formal religion. Everything that man touches seems sooner or later to become debased, and religion is no exception; instead of renewing ourselves day by day, our worship and prayers become mechanical, and so, instead of a life-giving force in our hearts, we carry a useless burden.

A terrible expression is used here—the Lord is *bored* by our worship of Him. "They are a trouble unto me; I am weary to bear them. And when ye spread forth your hands, I will hide mine eyes from you." If it is tiresome to hear a dull, mechanical sermon for half an hour, think what the Divine patience must be to hear all the prayers, hymns, and modes of worship! Apparently sinners do not begin to exhaust His patience so much as monotonous lip-service.

Remember, in the following passage Isaiah is speaking to the orthodox:

Wash you, make you clean; put away the evil of your doings from before mine eyes; cease to do evil; learn to do well; seek judgment, relieve the oppressed, judge the fatherless, plead for the widow.

Corruption had broken out in high places and, as sometimes happens, even in religious organisations, the camp-followers had come to the front.

Yet through all this fierce condemnation of hypocrisy and apostasy, there is in the book of the prophet Isaiah a belief in ultimate redemption; Israel has become disgraced and trodden down by foreign foes because of her own wickedness and cynicism; but she will be purified by humiliation, and out of these very people will come a Redeemer, not only for the Jews, but for the whole world. Like all great teachers of religion and morality, he believes that the soul of man is worth saving, and that it can be saved; he looks forward, as so many stout hearts have done, to a distant age of universal peace and brotherly love.

It is inspiring to remember that there has never been a time in history when the call to truth and righteousness was not heard; man cannot really live except through the life of the spirit. The spiritual is as much a part of human nature as selfish desires; and the eloquence of Isaiah is at once a witness to the hunger and thirst of the soul, and a means of satisfaction. Man cannot live by bread alone. In a world so full of intense need, the most important things can be bought without money and without price.

Our Lord did not hesitate to take the leadership of humanity prophesied by Isaiah; He read to the people about Him the words of the prophet, and then, with divine audacity, He said, in thrilling tones, *To-day is this scripture fulfilled in your ears.*

www.ingramcontent.com/pod-product-compliance
Lightning Source LLC
Chambersburg PA
CBHW031643040426
42453CB00006B/192